GEORGE SAMUEL

Courage in time of Discouragement

A Nuclear Scientist Speaks . . .

CHRISTIAN • LITERATURE • CRUSADE
Fort Washington, Pennsylvania 19034

CHRISTIAN LITERATURE CRUSADE

U.S.A.
P.O. Box 1449, Fort Washington, PA 19034

Copyright © Dr. George Samuel

First American Edition 1995

ISBN 0-87508-741-8

PRINTED IN THE UNITED STATES OF AMERICA

Contents

Foreword

Is your life constantly full of crises and difficulties? Do daily problems overwhelm you to the point where you just want to give up? Do you feel utterly alone in the midst of devastating circumstances which tend to pull you under, leaving you with little or no hope for tomorrow?

This book will offer you help in finding answers to the basic questions in your life. The solutions presented will not result in a life free of troubles and difficulties. Rather, the author has discovered a foundation in life that makes it possible to deal with massive daily problems. It is a foundation which cannot be removed, broken up or blown apart.

There are few people in this world who can remain gentle yet firm, warm but not hot, passionate but not fanatical. George Samuel is such a person and through his life experiences he has proven that there is indeed hope in life's darkest hours.

This book does not just deal with the problems in George Samuel's life; it offers solutions for your life as well. In this book you will find principles to transform your life, your family, and ultimately society itself.

As you read, may you be led to respond to those principles that the author has found helpful for himself.

Lars B. Dunberg
International President
Living Bibles International

Introduction

Over and over, several of my friends, both Christian and non-Christian, have asked me one question: "George, why don't you put some of your experiences on paper?" It is this continued interest that has finally motivated me to do as so many have suggested: write a book.

Most of the experiences I describe in these pages were devastating, particularly because I wasn't prepared for them. Yet, in the midst of the devastation, something beyond me often enabled me to accept what I faced and respond positively. When this happened, the difficult circumstances were transformed into an experience of joy and satisfaction.

Throughout the events in this book, I have seen people who handled their life situations courageously, subjecting their faith to the test of experience. (I've mentioned some of these people in the Epilogue.) And I learned many useful biblical principles from these men and women of God. Though I am still, at times, deficient in my responses, one fact has stood firm: through it all, I have seen a God who intervenes in all my affairs. It is He who makes the difference.

I always have loved to experiment, to test everything, including spiritual concepts and beliefs. I think my mind, trained for scientific inquiry, looks for proof—even for the existence of God! In this book, you will see that I have had many opportunities for such spiritual experiments.

However, while these experiences have helped me gain

valuable insights, I never allowed them to become my basis for forming principles or developing truths. Experiences alone can never be the criteria for truth; eternal principles and truths come only from God's Word. But these events *have* taught me that biblical truths can be confirmed in our daily experiences. We must not allow doubt and disappointment to discourage us. With God's help, we can turn tragedy into triumph, obstacles into opportunities, the worst into the best, and problems into projects that will have great and lasting value.

My family has been working alongside me, helping to prepare this manuscript for publication. My wife corrected the typographical errors. My two boys, Johny and Ronnie, helped me type the passages from *The Living Bible* accurately. Johny and Ronnie have cystic fibrosis, a condition for which no curative therapy is available. Our daughter, Annie, is the healthiest in the family right now. Ironically, she struggles with this because she ends up having to do much of the manual work. As you probably can imagine, our entire family has gone through many discouraging experiences together. Yet, time and again, God has brought us through it all.

Friends at Living Bibles International not only urged me to write some of these testimonies, they even offered their help in publishing the material. I would like to take this opportunity to express my thanks and deep appreciation to them, and to all who have helped in the publication of this book. As you read it, I hope you be able to see the same God who has been at work in my life working in your daily life situations as well. I know that our experiences are unique. We humans are not mass-produced; each of us is different. But we are all able to turn to the same Source, the One God, to receive courage in a world of discouragements.

George Samuel

1

Traveling With God

FAITH AND PRAYER REALLY WORK!

As a scientist, I travel a great deal for my work. Although I am fairly confident of finding my way around most places I visit, I always feel more comfortable and relaxed if someone meets me at the airport, railway station, or bus station. So it was that on August 28, 1985, I found myself waiting to meet my host at the Amsterdam Airport, where I had just arrived from Bombay.

The flight had been long and tiring. I had left Cochin the previous morning, waited at Bombay airport till midnight, and then flown to Amsterdam via Cairo. I wanted to have a good rest before my next appointment, so I was eagerly looking about the arrival area, trying to spot a person holding up a card or some sort of indicator with my name on it. I wanted to make it as easy as possible for my contact to find me among the bustle of arriving passengers.

Before long, I began to feel a little uneasy. I couldn't see anyone waiting for me. *Perhaps no one is going to meet me,* I thought. *Or maybe my contact has been delayed.* With a tired sigh, I decided to find my own way to the hotel.

I reviewed my alternatives, including making a phone call—which would mean moving my luggage to the telephone booth and risking the possibility that my contact would miss me. While I was trying to decide what to do, I spotted a van from my hotel maneuvering between cars. Not wanting to waste further time, I made for the van, knowing that hotel transportation is always safer for a stranger.

To my dismay, when I arrived at the hotel I discovered that they were fully booked and my name was not on the waiting list. I found a phone, called my office, and was informed that a booking had been made for me in another hotel. Unhappily, I realized that if I had waited patiently for the host to meet me at the airport, he would have taken me to the right hotel. My only choice now was to get to the other hotel, which—fortunately—was only a couple of kilometers away.

I hailed a taxi in front of the hotel. The driver was quite helpful. He loaded my baggage and helped me into the vehicle. As he sped along, I felt thankful he wanted to give me such a quick ride. *I can get a shower, breakfast, and even take my blood pressure medication in no time,* I thought with relief. *If I get some good rest in before noon, I will be ready for my afternoon appointment.*

Suddenly the taxi pulled to a stop. But when I looked up, I saw that instead of taking me to the hotel, the taxi driver had driven to a deserted place. I knew I was in danger. As I watched, the driver reached up and tugged at his hair, which fell away in his hand—he had been wearing a wig! Then he briskly opened a briefcase he had on the front seat. Fear jolted through me when I saw what it contained: a gun, a knife, and a syringe—probably filled with a poison or a drug.

I wanted to get out of the taxi, but the driver would not let me. Instead he searched me and the contents of my suitcase thoroughly. The only money I had was twenty guilders, which is worth less than $7.00. The man was disappointed and vented his frustration over "kidnapping the wrong person." He grew quite angry with me, my luggage, and his car. At first it seemed he did not know what to do with me. He probably realized that he would end up behind bars if he released me. His only option was to get rid of me.

He drove onto the expressway, probably with the intention of killing me and throwing my body into one of the canals. No matter what I said, he would not listen to me. In desperation, I opened the left rear door, stretched out my arm and shouted for help, trying to alert someone in one of the passing vehicles. It was no use. No one noticed my frantic efforts. When the robber realized I was trying to alert others, he became furious and reached for his gun. I gave up my efforts to get help. I even asked him to forgive my foolishness, hoping a friendly approach would be better.

What is the best approach when your life is in danger? Who is there to give you counsel? Already I had had a sleepless night of air travel. In addition, I was on blood pressure medication, which I had not taken yet. I was physically tired and mentally and emotionally distressed. I couldn't even remember the things I had learned in counseling about dealing with distraught or dangerous people. I was at a loss as to what to do.

Suddenly I heard a whispering inside me: *"Son, don't you know that many people are praying for you right now?"* A sense of calm began to fill me. My family and many people around the world pray for me regularly. Being reminded about this intercessory prayer was comforting and encouraging.

With this assurance, I leaned forward and spoke boldly to the robber. "Look! Many people are praying for me. You cannot kill me! Please take me to the hotel I told you to drive me to!" He didn't even respond. I continued to talk to him, seemingly without any effect. Finally I said, "I am going to join them in prayer as well. You cannot kill me."

As I bowed my head in prayer, I was reminded of the way God had delivered Daniel from the lions' den, and how Paul and others in the ship taking him to Rome were delivered from the shipwreck. Then a part of the prayer my son Ronnie had said just before I left on my trip came to my mind: "Lord, may none of the assaults of the evil one come near us." I was greatly strengthened. My fear of that gun and knife vanished. I sat in the back seat of that taxi and continued praying—praying to the One who hears our prayers. I knew without a doubt that God had heard the prayers of my family and friends. He had spoken to me through that inner voice to confirm this to me.

Another soothing thought came to me while I sat there praying. I recalled a Bible verse my grandmother taught me when I was four years old: "Even though I walk through the valley of the shadow of death, I fear no evil; for thou art with me." In *The Living Bible,* this verse reads: "Even when walking through the dark valley of death I will not be afraid, for you are close beside me, guarding, guiding all the way" (Psalm 23:4).

Though my situation was frightening, that Bible verse calmed me. I felt Someone close beside me, guarding me. It was as if the Lord was sitting and riding with me! That was so precious.

So often I had read promises such as, "I am with you always, even to the end of the world" (Matthew 28:20), and "God is our refuge and strength, a tested help in times of trouble. And so we need not fear even if the world blows up" (Psalm 46:1–2). Now I knew God's promises were real; they are there for us to use. They are relevant and meaningful, and they can bring us peace in the midst of fear.

That is exactly what they did for me that night.

Suddenly, I wanted to share that peace. Instead of commanding or cursing the driver, I tried to become his friend. I talked to him about the One who was sitting with me in his cab. Again he did not respond, he just kept driving—fast. But I was not distressed. Terms like "the dark valley of death" and "God is close beside me guarding me" were echoing inside me. I continued praying, and my prayers in that dingy cab were more meaningful than any I had prayed in a beautiful cathedral. It was a life-and-death affair for me, yet what I felt inside was peace.

Finally, the robber spoke, his gruff voice breaking the silence. "If you assure me you will not report me to the police, I will release you."

"I will be very grateful if you would do that," I replied, immensely thankful. I was ready to get out right there on the roadside, even if it meant leaving my baggage with him. I told him so.

"No, I will take you to the hotel," he said in a soft voice.

He turned the cab and suddenly I knew we were heading for the hotel instead of to the dark valley of death. When we were still a little distance away, the robber pointed out the hotel to reassure me. At long last, he pulled to a stop.

"Don't get out or open the door," he instructed as he opened his door and got out. I obeyed him. I saw him carrying my baggage to the hotel lobby. "Leave all the money you have on the front seat," he said when he returned. I informed him I only had twenty guilders with me, which was sufficient to pay the fare for the original five-minute ride. I handed him the money with gratitude, and he then escorted me to the front lobby and pushed me inside the reception area where he had left my baggage. Then he was gone.

I felt almost weak with relief. Oh, I am not afraid of

death; I am immortal until my work is done. After my work on this planet is finished, there is no point in remaining here. But I did not feel that my work was done, and I was grateful to know that God agreed!

When I was finally in my hotel room getting ready for a shower, I began to relive that taxi ride. The more I thought about it, the more I thanked the Lord. After the shower, I began to imagine my body floating in that canal water and my family waiting for my return . . . what terrible pain and distress my disappearance would have caused among family and friends. Once again I thanked God for his intervention and protection.

Looking back, I know that what controlled this dangerous situation was prayer. Whether we go through dangerous experiences or not, God hears our prayers. Prayer is an expression of our faith in God, and we show our love toward others when we pray for people and their needs.

When we pray, we have the assurance that God is listening. I can pray boldly. Even if I am not sure how to pray, I can know that prayer is a spiritual exercise and that God's Holy Spirit is decoding my words, making them acceptable to God.

I remember, for example, when my daughter Annie was one-and-a-half years old. She used to crawl to the dining table where we kept a pretty, double-edged knife for cutting bread and other items. One day Annie asked me for the knife so that she could play with it. As a loving father, I sensed her real desire—to play with something pretty—and so I gave her a brand new toy. Though Annie had asked for a knife, which would have been dangerous in the little hands of a child, what she really wanted was a toy. I "decoded" her request, and gave her what was best for her.

Likewise, our prayers are decoded by the Spirit. Even though we are not always sure how to pray, we can still ask, believing that God will give us only the best (see Romans 8:26).

God wants so much to care for us in all we face. Too often we don't realize that! Nor do we realize the many ways God is able to help us. In Luke 8:23–24, we read of an incident when Jesus was with His disciples in a boat. Suddenly "a fierce storm developed that threatened to swamp them, and they were in real danger. . . . 'Master, Master, we are sinking!' they screamed. So he [Jesus] spoke to the storm: 'Quiet down,' he said, and the wind and waves subsided and all was calm!" (Luke 8:23–24). Those disciples had already experienced the presence of Jesus; now they experienced His power.

Many people wonder if we can also experience that power today. There is so much evil in the world. We have to overcome many unpleasant, and sometimes dangerous, situations. We find it difficult to overcome with only our own strength. How wonderful that we do not need to do so! God not only gives us the strength we need, but He also comforts and encourages us! He knows our anxiety and fear. In fact, Jesus came to dwell with man to know our pain, fear, and anxiety. That was one of the purposes of the incarnation—of God becoming man: "Since he himself has now been through suffering and temptation, he knows what it is like when we suffer and are tempted, and he is wonderfully able to help us" (Hebrews 2:18).

God's power is available to each of us. He waits to enable us to overcome every dangerous situation we will ever face. The grace that enabled Jesus to walk through the world overcoming all difficulties and problems is able to support us and sustain us today. I know this for a fact—I have experienced it firsthand!

I later found out that the person sent to meet my flight at the Amsterdam airport had, indeed, been delayed. If I had made my own arrangements, I would have planned beforehand without making any on-the-spot decision. If I had known earlier about the hotel reservations, I would have made foolproof arrangements. But things seldom work as we expect them to. We face risks every day. But the greatest—and best—risk any of us can take is that of trusting God and believing that He will fulfill His promises to us!

God Is Sufficient

In July of 1960, I was asked to appear for a job interview on a Thursday. The invitation reached me by telegram on the Sunday afternoon just before the interview. Before that time, I had never traveled outside of the state of Kerala. Now, suddenly, I had to travel all the way to Bombay, 1,900 kilometers (1,200 miles) away. Since this would be the first time I would deal with trains, train trips, and names of railway stations, I decided I did not want to do it all alone. I hunted up the address of a schoolmate who had gone to Bombay a few years earlier. On my way to the railway station at Cochin Harbour Terminus, I stopped by a telegraph office and sent a telegram to my friend's post office box.

Not until I purchased the ticket at Cochin did I realize that I would be reaching Bombay Victoria Terminus station and not Bombay Central station, which is where I had asked my schoolmate to meet me. As you can imagine, I prayed a great deal as I considered the long, three-day train ride ahead of me. I wondered how I would find a place to stay in Bombay when I finally arrived since I had told my friend to meet me at the wrong railway station.

The more I tried to picture Bombay, and the more I thought about stories of strangers being cheated in large cities, the more powerful my prayer became. Since I was traveling in a "through compartment to Bombay," the possibilities for finding someone along the way to help me were limited. Furthermore, I didn't want strangers on the train to know I wouldn't have anyone to meet me or look after me when I reached my final destination.

My parents and grandparents had taught me to pray for everything. Throughout my life, I had seen prayer work in the lives of at least a few people. So it was only natural for me to pray now. I prayed for protection while I was on the train and when I reached Bombay, and I prayed for the interview.

However, I began to grow fearful as we got closer to Bombay. In casual conversations with my fellow passengers, I tried to find out as much information about Bombay as possible—especially the way to find accommodations and to move around in the city.

I tried to figure out how to find the street address for my friend's post office box. But even if I found it there would be no point in going to the post office in search of my friend. It was not likely he would be standing at his post office box, waiting for me! Still, prayer sustained me through my worries. When the train came to a halt, I stepped down onto the platform at Victoria Terminus with great courage.

Suddenly I felt a man's touch on my shoulder, and heard a voice asking, "How was the train trip?" Amazed, I turned to see my friend holding my telegram in his hand! I thanked the Lord for hearing my prayer. I hadn't even had to look around for someone coming to meet me. My friend's appearance had been perfectly timed.

"How did you know I would arrive at Victoria Terminus?" I asked.

My friend smiled. "It was really amazing. I changed my job a long time ago, so the post office box where you sent your telegram was my old office address. But this morning I felt like taking a half-day leave, and something inside prompted me to visit my old office. I had just arrived there when the receptionist handed me your telegram! It said you were arriving today at Bombay Central station, but the time given was for the arrival of this train, which brings passengers from Kerala. So I thought I'd better come and look for you here first."

I did not have to wonder who had prompted my friend to take a half-day off that morning. Nor who had prompted him to visit his old office without any special reason. The answer was clear: the One God who cares for us and watches over us had heard my prayers and answered! My friend took me to get something to eat and made sure I could have a bath to clean up from the long journey. Then he set up accommodations for me with good friends, and even showed me the building where I would go the next morning for the interview.

As I sank into bed that night, I was filled with wonder at the way everything had been arranged for me, a stranger who was so timid and fearful. Surely the One who knew my anxiety and fear wanted to show me His power. God is more concerned about my safety than I am. "Let him have all your worries and cares, for he is always thinking about you and watching everything that concerns you" (1 Peter 5:7).

I had been imagining all kinds of dangers and fearful situations when I realized that my way of handling the situation had gone wrong. But the Bible says: "Don't worry about anything; instead, pray about everything; tell God your needs and don't forget to thank him for his answers" (Philippians 4:6).

God not only hears our prayers, He also provides for us in wonderful ways. Jesus said: "Let not your heart be troubled . . . trust in me" (John 14:1). There is no need to be worried and upset. We can believe the One who is always thinking about us. Sometimes God sends someone to meet your train right on time and saves you from worries and cares. Other times, God may delay the person and allow you to go through an anxious period. The choice is not ours. But I am happy with the choice of our sovereign God. I want to believe in and trust Him and serve Him regardless of His choice.

2

Peace in the
Middle of the Storms

NEWS NO PARENT WANTS TO HEAR

In the early seventies I was responsible for setting up and running a nuclear medicine department at Bay Harbor Hospital in Harbor City, California. At that time my wife and two children were still living in Kerala.

In the course of my work at Bay Harbor, I met many of the hospital's patients and their relatives, as well as a number of clinical and nonclinical staff members. I enjoyed working with these people, and tried to provide the best services possible to the community. As a result, I gained people's confidence and got to know their thought forms, life-styles, and values.

Because medical insurance was provided by the patients' employers, many people made use of the hospital's facility to take care of their medical problems. Understandably, everyone wanted to get negative reports from the diagnostic studies done in my department. But when tests did have positive results, we in the department would have discussions with the respective specialists.

One day as we were discussing a couple of bone cancer cases, I was told I had a telephone call. The message was a cable, relayed over the telephone, from Kerala. I knew that both of my sons had been ill. The older boy, who was nearly three years old, was especially ill. As I listened to the cable, I heard news no parent ever wants to hear: my younger son had died. After I received the message, I returned to my colleagues to finish the discussion, which took another twenty minutes. When it was over, I told my colleagues about the death of my son.

They were shocked. They couldn't believe I had come back from this sudden, devastating news to continue participating in our discussion. Their love, empathy, and condolences were expressed by a pin-drop silence. I finally broke that silence by telling the group that I had been able to go on because I had experienced "God's peace, which is far more wonderful than the human mind can understand." Yes, that peace "will keep your thoughts and your hearts quiet and at rest" (Philippians 4:7). That wonderful peace, which I had heard about for years, filled me that day and gave me the strength to do what I needed to do, despite the terrible loss I had suffered.

There are those who are skeptical about the existence of a "peace that transcends all understanding." New knowledge is being gained every day. In fact, one calculation states that it would take five years for an average student to complete reading all the new knowledge that is accumulated during every twenty-four-hour period! It is practically impossible for the human mind to comprehend something that transcends *all* understanding.

And yet, at that moment of my greatest need, I experienced such a peace—a peace that kept "my thoughts and heart quiet and at rest." Jesus said, "I am leaving you with a gift—peace of mind and heart! And the peace I give isn't fragile like the peace the world gives. So don't be troubled or afraid" (John 14:27).

When I finally left my colleagues, I wanted to find out the details of my child's death. Those days it was difficult to get telephone connections to our hometown in Kerala. I booked an overseas call to Tiruvalla, my hometown in India, thinking that I might get through during the night. I reminded the overseas operator about my pending call after I had eaten my evening meal.

In a few minutes, I heard my telephone ringing. I answered it eagerly, hoping it was my wife. But it was a local call from a troubled man I have helped and encouraged now and then. He was going through a difficult time, struggling with feelings of depression, and he asked if I would counsel him. After talking to him for more than thirty minutes, he thanked me and asked me to pray for him. I prayed a short prayer; then, as I was saying "good night," I asked him to pray for me, too.

"What's the matter?" he asked.

"This morning I received a cable message from home in India informing me that my younger son has died. I've booked a telephone call to speak to my wife and will appreciate your prayers that the call will go through soon," I explained.

Suddenly he began to weep like a baby. "Your problem is bigger than mine," he said, "but you took so much of your valuable time to help me. It seems you even forgot that you were waiting for the overseas call." He continued weeping.

"The God who enabled me to help you is able to solve all your problems," I responded. I did not begrudge the time I had spent talking with this man. I knew that if we nurse only our own wounds, we will not be able to see the wounds of others. And that is what Christ calls us to: seeing and helping to heal the wounds of others.

I told the weeping man to trust God and not to worry.

God was not only going to take care of his needs but was also going to bless others through him—and I told him that I was actually strengthened by taking the time to help another who was in pain.

My call to India went through around midnight, and before going to bed I thanked the Lord for all He had done in my life that day.

"What a wonderful God we have . . . the source of every mercy, and the one who so wonderfully comforts and strengthens us in our hardships and trials. And why does he do this? So that when others are troubled, needing our sympathy and encouragement, we can pass on to them this same help and comfort God has given us" (2 Corinthians 1:3–4).

God tenderly comforts us when we suffer. Even more, though, He helps us use such times to apply what He has taught us, to use our insights and learning for the benefit of others. We know that this world is full of suffering. We encounter many opportunities to help others with the courage we gain from our own afflictions. "We can rejoice, too, when we run into problems and trials for we know that they are good for us—they help us learn to be patient. And patience develops strength of character in us and helps us trust God more each time we use it until finally our hope and faith are strong and steady" (Romans 5:3–4).

We not only bear suffering and frustration, but we utilize them to turn our tragedy into triumph. The one thing that enables us to do this is that God has more than enough grace to meet our special needs, regardless of circumstances.

"NIGHT STAY" TURNED OUT TO BE "NICE DAY!"

When I travel, I normally use air travel to save time—

which can make flight delays very frustrating. Once on my way to Madras, I had a stopover in Colombo. Suddenly the chief steward announced over the public address system that there would be a delay of several hours. That meant we would have to have a "night stay" in Colombo. The passengers were sure they couldn't have heard correctly, because it was only 9 A.M.! Several began to complain and grumble. Some started getting angry. No one was willing to move out of the airport area.

While we were waiting for transportation to the hotel, I decided to put Proverbs 12:25 into action: "Anxious hearts are very heavy but a word of encouragement does wonders!" I looked around and shouted: "We are going to have a *nice day* here, not a *night stay!* That's what *I* heard them say."

The airline put us up in a five-star hotel, where we enjoyed free meals. And we went sight-seeing. Then, around 5:30 P.M., we were told that the ground engineers had repaired the radar equipment of the aircraft, and we were all called back to resume our flight. As it turned out, we really *did* have a *nice day* instead of a *night stay*. God's grace can help change attitudes.

Sometimes we feel powerless to change our attitude. But when we change our thoughts, we change the world around us. It's true that we don't have strength within us to counteract the strong influence of certain situations. That is the time we must turn to God for help. In God, we have great power; that's why we say that with God's grace we can change the worst into the best. Dr. John Haggai has taught me the definition of grace. He said, "Grace is God giving us freely what He requires of us." God wants me to change my attitude. Since I don't have the power to do that myself, God, by grace, gives me the power to do it.

THE CASE OF THE STOLEN BRIEFCASE

Several years ago, in September of 1982, I was at the airport in Lima, Peru. I didn't want to bother my host by asking him to stay with me at the check-in area at the airport. So I asked my host to drop me at the departure area and go home to have some rest instead of waiting on me till I got into the immigration area.

I stood in line along with the other passengers, holding onto my briefcase and pushing the suitcase forward until it was my turn. When I got to the counter, I requested a good seat as it was a night flight from Lima to Los Angeles. I handed the agent my tickets, passport, and the ten-dollar airport tax. All the other documents—my health certificate against yellow fever, Bible, notes, glasses, items for personal use, and money—were in my briefcase, which is allowed as a hand-carried bag.

Then disaster struck! During the few seconds I was talking to the agent at the check-in counter, someone stole my briefcase! I thought I had been watching it carefully, but apparently I hadn't been careful enough. I approached the airline staff and the local police. They responded in Spanish—probably telling me that I would never see my briefcase again. Finally I decided to telephone my host so that I could at least block the traveler's checks from being used. But my glasses were in the briefcase, and I couldn't find the telephone number because of the small print.

The airline staff showed me some sympathy, however, and offered me a cool drink to quench my thirst. As I sat and sipped the drink, I began to wonder how, without the certificate for yellow fever, I was going to enter the U.S.A. after having visited South America. Thankfully, an airline official gave me a letter explaining the loss of my health certificate, which would be sufficient.

Traveling empty-handed was a strange experience for me. I knew that anxiety and frustration could lead to fear and depression, and could even cause me to get sick. So I didn't want to get bogged down in worry over the loss of property and valuable documents. Although my hand was empty, my heart was full of assurance and hope. Bible verses like "Always be full of joy in the Lord; I say it again, rejoice" (Philippians 4:4), and "Always give thanks for everything to our God" (Ephesians 5:20) kept coming to mind. I began to see that we have to rejoice and praise God even for losses. When we praise God in the midst of loss, we acknowledge that He will compensate us for the loss. God never takes away the good and desirable things from our hand unless He is going to replace them with something far better!

Once I made it home, I had to replace the Bible and practically all the materials I used for travel, including the briefcase itself. Of course, the Lord taught me to be more careful, and I even told my other friends who are used to such travel what had happened to caution them against overconfidence.

Several days later I thought I would be able to trace the thief when the bank informed me that a traveler's check was cashed through an account holder in a South American bank. I was surprised to see the copy of my forged signature. The thief must have copied my signature from the health certificate. I corresponded a great deal with the bank, but they weren't cooperative in tracing the thief. I was just grateful that my air ticket (all the way to Trivandrum, India) and passport weren't in the briefcase when it was stolen.

God worked on my attitude toward the thief. Thieves are surely needy people. We have to love even the antisocial elements of our world. We must always remember that

Jesus came to save sinners. Yes, our Lord hates sin, but He loves sinners. Whether someone commits sin as a victim of circumstances or does it willfully, Jesus still prays the prayer: "Father, forgive these people . . . for they don't know what they are doing" (Luke 23:34).

God reminded me that Jesus is praying not only for people who steal, but for me also. I need to be forgiven for my wrong attitude that I show in my responses. In God's mercy, we all receive the forgiveness we need. But confessing our faults and sins and receiving forgiveness isn't a license to do it again.

I was told of one boy who lived in a community hostel. He confessed to the warden that he had stolen three apples from the kitchen store. But the kitchen staff found only two missing when counted. The boy was questioned about the third apple mentioned in his confession. He replied that he would steal the third one the following week and so confessed in advance.

Admit before God your desire to avoid sin and confess your sins. The apostle Paul said: ". . . I used to scoff at the name of Christ. I hunted down his people, harming them in every way I could. But God had mercy on me because I didn't know what I was doing, for I didn't know Christ at that time. Oh, how kind our Lord was, for he showed me how to trust him" (1 Timothy 1:13–14).

It's easy for us to think we really don't do anything that needs forgiveness. But we all are human, and we all sin. When you are lazy or waste time at your job, you are actually stealing from your employers. When you do personal things during office hours, you are stealing from your employer. If you aren't giving a certain portion of your income, say ten percent or so, to God's work, you are stealing what belongs to God. Here, too, you may have to get right with God.

God used this experience and my feelings about the thief to help me see that we all need forgiveness. None of us is blameless. But we all can be forgiven!

A Theft From a Locked Car

Seven years later, on August 28, 1989, I had another bag stolen. This time I had my bag with me in a car on my way to the railway station from Cochin airport. When both the car owner and I left the car to run an errand, a thief broke open the rear door and stole my bag. It contained my Bible, prayer diary, notes, files, papers I had been working on for an upcoming Living Bibles International board meeting, reimbursement money for the air ticket, clothes, alarm clock, medicine for my blood pressure, and other personal items.

We had left the car parked on a busy street and had been away only fifteen minutes. But that had been enough time for the thief to get his "job" done. This time I was more calm and relaxed, probably because my bag was stolen by one of my own countrymen. I had to take the next train home, so I didn't have time to report the theft to the police. I didn't curse the thief, although I didn't agree with his way of getting my things. Instead, I sang. "Sing and praise and worship the Lord." Again, I wanted to give thanks at all times for all things. I had sufficient money for the train fare, so I found a seat where I could relax and sing in my heart.

After a while I went to sleep (which I could do with confidence because I had no bag to watch!). Later, I thought about my Bible and the prayer diary in which various prayer needs were listed on a daily and weekly basis. I have many people to pray for, so I use a written list to remember them faithfully. I started visualizing the pages of the prayer diary in order to make another one. I also started to make a new address and telephone book. I felt calm and peaceful—what a blessed difference from what could have been! Instead of being anxious or angry about my loss, I simply began concentrating on what I needed to replace so I could continue my work and ministry.

Another blessing in the midst of this situation was that I didn't suffer any negative physical reactions to the loss of my bag. In the past, I used to suffer a terrible thirst if something like this happened. I would have to drink a lot of water soon after facing such situations. This time, I only had one cup of tea at the railway station. My body chemistry seemed unaffected.

Singing praises to God came to me spontaneously. That song was meaningful to me, and I realized I wasn't singing it out of some nervous hysteria. I was singing out of love and gratitude to my Lord.

Some dear friends were eager to replace the money I had lost, and I was so grateful to them for their generosity. However, I did regret losing those items that money cannot replace. But even those feelings became a blessing as I grew grateful that my parents and some of my teachers had given me valuable things that money cannot buy, gifts that could never be stolen, such as character and integrity. But in my bag I had a few notebooks in which I had written several valuable insights and other papers that I needed urgently. I prayed that God someday would bring these things back to me. I know there is nothing wrong with asking God to give back to you something that you have lost. After all, our God is a God of impossibilities.

I received a letter exactly one month later from the manager of a tourist lodge, informing me that a bag had been left in one of their rooms. Because the manager found my address on some papers inside the bag, he wrote to me. When I collected my bag, I found that only the money and a few items of personal use were gone. My Bible, prayer diary, notebooks, glasses, all the papers, and even the envelope used for wrapping the money was left. The items that were taken can be replaced. I praise God for returning to me all the items that money could never replace.

This theft taught me to be more cautious. True, God watches over us, but we shouldn't try to make our God a watchdog or detective agent. We have to take care of our own belongings. Of course, even when we are careful we may make mistakes or be victimized. Being Christians doesn't give us any special insulation against the various attacks of our society and world. Sometimes God preserves us; other times, we must suffer as anyone else. Is this fair? Consider the story of three men of God who lived at the time of King Nebuchadnezzar:

So they bound them tight with ropes and threw them into the furnace, fully clothed. And because the king, in his anger, had demanded such a hot fire in the furnace, the flames leaped out and killed the soldiers as they threw them in! So Shadrach, Meshach, and Abednego fell down bound into the roaring flames.

But suddenly, as he was watching, Nebuchadnezzar jumped up in amazement and exclaimed to his advisors, "Didn't we throw three men into the furnace?"

"Yes," they said, "we did indeed, Your Majesty."

. . . Then Nebuchadnezzar came as close as he could to the open door of the flaming furnace and yelled: "Shadrach, Meshach, and Abednego, servants of the Most High God! Come out! Come here!" So they stepped out of the fire.

Then the Princes saw that the fire hadn't touched them—not a hair of their heads was singed; their coats were unscorched, and they didn't even smell of smoke! (Daniel 3:21–27).

Usually, fire burns. But God can use or even bypass the natural process. It is His choice. Whatever God decides, we will find peace and joy when we obey Him and love Him. God wants us to glorify Him whether our belongings are lost or miraculously found.

It may be that you are perplexed over many matters; that there seem to be no solutions to your problems. Or it may be that you committed some troubling or perplexing matters to God in prayer and you are still not able to find any solutions. Or perhaps you tried your level best to protect yourself from any calamities and still unpleasant things happened. Or you may have recently experienced a "bypass" moment—when you found the perfect solution quickly, or unexpectedly had stolen items returned, or had a sickness healed even before you started taking the prescribed medication!

Whatever your situation, whether it is receiving answers to prayer or not receiving answers, always remember that the glory goes to God. God *wants* us to glorify Him. Don't think that God is selfish when He demands that we give Him the glory. He only asks us to give Him that which He deserves.

What do we mean by glorifying God? Read on into the next chapter to gain some insights into this.

3

All the Proof You Need

THE IMPORTANCE OF QUESTIONS

Questions have played an important part in my life. I have been asked many different questions by many different people. Some people were seeking immediate answers. Others hoped to learn something from my experiences. A few questioned me simply out of curiosity. My friends often ask me questions because they know I enjoy being asked, especially when the questions are in my area of specialty.

But there was one question that I had been asking myself for a very long time: "Where does *God* fit into the system of electrons and nucleus of the atom or the system of planets and stars and galaxies of the universe?" From this question came my drive to find some kind of proof of the existence of God.

My parents and grandparents brought me up in a godly home. Intense belief in God was a must in our home. We all prayed seriously and participated regularly in spiritual exercises.

Then I became a keen student of science, and suddenly my faith in God was shaken! In science classes I gained much knowledge from lectures. In my lab times I would experiment to see the proof of my theories. I learned to put my scientific thoughts and theories to the test. Likewise, I began to see that I needed to subject my religious beliefs to the test of experience. I was satisfied with the evidences I found in my science classes, but the one thing I couldn't find was a satisfactory explanation or any proof for the existence of God.

My parents advised me to read my Bible and pray regularly. But to whom do you pray when you are in doubt? Then I thought, *Suppose there is a God, and I do not pray; perhaps something bad might happen to me. It is best to pray to be on the safe side.* But I knew it was almost intellectual suicide to pray and at the same time deny the existence of God. The best way to pray, therefore, was to say in the beginning, "If after all there is a God, let Him hear."

I continued praying and reading my Bible every day. One evening I came upon a passage in the Bible: "Unless you are born again, you can never get into the Kingdom of God" (John 3:3). The term *born again* kept coming into my mind, nagging at me, troubling me. Finally I decided to get my mind on other things, and I began to concentrate on some math assignments.

But still this matter of becoming born again kept coming back into my mind—along with various sermons I had heard on this topic in meetings and Sunday School classes, and what I heard from parents and grandparents! I couldn't get it out of my mind. I began to wonder if something wasn't wrong with me, and that that was why I found it difficult to accept spiritual reality or God.

The funny thing is that I was right without knowing it. There *was* something wrong with me: my sins! I was trying to get the approval of my parents, relatives, friends and teachers, and I was leading a clean life. I was like the pickpocket I had once heard about in a sermon. The minister spoke of a pickpocket who went to the bus station intending to relieve the people there of their money. However, once there he found that all of his intended victims were careful about their pockets and money, and he had no success. So he went home in the evening and said to himself, "I did not commit the sin of stealing this day." Surely, he didn't commit the act of stealing because he didn't get the opportunity to do so. But he had already sinned—through his intent—in his heart.

I, too, had often felt I wasn't a sinner. After all, I hadn't really done sinful things. But that night I realized I *was* a sinner. And I began to see that I found it difficult to believe in God not because God doesn't exist, but because something was wrong with me—my sins. And with this realization came another: I needed someone to take away my guilt feelings. I remembered learning in Sunday School classes that Jesus is able to clean up everything because of what He did on the cross for our sins. That night I knew I wanted to try Jesus. I decided to subject this offer of forgiveness and cleansing to the test of experience. How wonderful that in my search for proof of God's existence, the first proof I discovered was the transformation that God produced in my own life. From that point, everything about me began to change.

I wanted to share with my friends what had happened, but I didn't want anyone to misunderstand me. So I decided to go slow on making any public statement about this transformation. It wasn't long, though, before I began to sense that my friends noticed a change in my behavior and responses. I overheard them talking to one another, saying there was something different about me, about my behavior, my attitude, and even the way I talked. I was thrilled! If my friends were seeing a change in me, that meant my transformation had been real. After that, I began to share boldly about the entire experiment.

This became another changing point for me, the point at which I began to experience God's love in my relationship with God, my friends, and myself. It was a radical redirection of my motives and interests in life.

Several years later, I taught about the production of nontoxic and short-lived radioisotopes used in medicine. I told my class about the change occurring on a target material bombarded with neutrons in the nuclear reactor. Those who listened to me knew I had actually had firsthand experience with such reactor-produced radioisotopes. They knew that I was telling them something real and tangible. None of them questioned the existence of the radioisotope because it is real and detectable. I could share my experience with confidence.

In the same way, I can tell about another transformation that is even more lasting and real. The life span of those reactor-produced radioisotopes is small; they die down fairly quickly. But when you experience a spiritual transformation, you enter into an eternal relationship with God. This transformation is real, powerful, and never-ending.

ANOTHER LIFE-CHANGING QUESTION

As I mentioned before, I have heard many questions in my life. In fact, I've heard so many that I have forgotten most of them. Except one. Not long after my transformation, a man I respected very much asked me a question that I have never forgotten: "What is the purpose of your life?"

I answered that I would like to become a nuclear scientist who would find a cure for the effects of nuclear weapons.

Obviously, I knew little of nuclear weapons. But I had become determined to fulfill this goal when I read a newspaper report of the first thermonuclear explosion of the hydrogen bomb. I was only fourteen years old at that time. The newspaper reporter explained all the possible havoc that could result from nuclear explosions. I determined in my young mind to develop a cure for the harmful effects of this terrible, destructive weapon. Since then, my interest as a budding research scientist had been to invent some kind of tablet that one could take to nullify the effects of nuclear weapons. I thought, most sincerely, that people who took my preventative medicine would be able to walk through the radiation, fallout, etc.

The man who had questioned me considered my answer thoughtfully. Then he said, "The purpose of our life is to glorify God." I looked at him in surprise as he went on. He explained that we should seek, above all, to glorify God by a life that's utterly devoted to serving Him. I remember thinking, *I'm already doing that. I am praying regularly and worshiping God and glorifying Him.* After all, I regularly said "Glory be to Thee, O God" three times during worship services.

This dear man then asked me questions about my work. I told him I was a student and that my work was studying. He then asked me whether I was glorifying God by my studies. I told him that I was scoring good marks for every test and remarked: "What more can one do for God's glory?"

"Are you studying merely for good grades or studying for God?" he asked. I knew I was studying for good grades. I knew how to select the kinds of questions that probably would be asked and then study the answers instead of learning the entire text. I got good grades using that method, but I didn't realize that I was cheating myself and God. This man helped me to learn that I wasn't glorifying God by my studies.

That conversation is something I have never forgotten. It became the turning point in my life, in my attitude toward work and toward my studies. "Whatever you do, do everything as if you are doing it for God" was the concept strongly injected in me.

I can now look back and say how this marvelous truth worked in my life. Of course, the adjustment wasn't easy. I remember one night, during my evening prayers, when I examined the day's events. On several occasions I got up, switched on the light, and read the pages in my textbook that I had earlier left unread because they were unimportant so far as the examination was concerned. I had to discipline myself to do everything as if I was doing it for God. But it was the right thing to do. I not only received good grades, I also learned a great deal about my different subjects.

This lesson has carried over into my work, too. In the Bible we read, "Be a good workman, one who doesn't need to be ashamed when God examines your work" (2 Timothy 2:15). To this very day, I seek to be the kind of workman in my profession and in my life who will make God proud of me. What greater reward could there be than that?

The Old, the New, and the Spiritual

I am glad I was asked about the purpose of my life soon after my born-again experience. It wouldn't have made any sense to me if someone had asked me about glorifying God when my faith in God was shaken and my heart was full of doubts. Now not only are those doubts gone, but I have become partaker of the new life that God gave me as a gift.

Sadly, this world is full of opposing forces. I want to glorify God, but there are a lot of things that get in the way. When all those storms of temptations crowd around me, I can turn to Someone to help me in my struggle between the old nature and the new nature. The old, sinful nature cannot be removed from my personality, but I can—with God's help—make that sin-loving nature unresponsive.

Think of someone who has just died. No matter what you say—whether it's accolades for all the good things the person did when he was alive or whether it's a list of all the terrible things he did—that corpse will not get up and respond. The Bible says, "So look upon your old sinful nature as dead and unresponsive to sin" (Romans 6:11). When temptations approach you in various forms, consider your old nature dead.

Of course, we can't do this on our own. But we don't have to. When we grow vegetables in our garden, some plants aren't strong enough to stand the storms, so we tie the plant to a strong support dug into the ground. The plant can now stand a storm, not because of its own strength but because of the strength of the support. Similarly, you and I receive strong support in God when we become born again. We are bound to Him through Christ Jesus, and nothing can ever separate us. He will be there when the storms hit—and He will help us survive.

A MIND LIKE CHRIST

Sports are a big part of life in the U.S.—and worldwide, too. We appreciate athletes who win. We even develop a great deal of respect for certain players who are especially good at what they do. However, suppose you wanted to perform like these star athletes, and so you observed their styles, manners, and methods closely, hoping to learn something.

But observing, taking lessons, practicing, or even eating the same kind of food usually will not enable you to perform like a star athlete. Probably the only way for you to become as proficient as this athlete would be to transplant his or her mind into your head. For it is in the *mind* that true change is made.

The Bible tells us, "Actually [we] do have within us a portion of the very thoughts and mind of Christ" (1 Corinthians 2:16). It makes a lot of difference when you have Christ living in you. When we are born again, we "have been crucified with Christ: and [we ourselves] no longer live, but Christ lives in [us]" (Galatians 2:20). We experience a spiritual transplant.

I knew this when I accepted Christ. But I realized only later that I have to live a "daily crucified" life. When Christ was crucified, His feet—which He had used to walk to needy people and help them—were immobilized. His hands—which He had used to touch many and bring healing and consolation—were nailed. His enemies thought He would never again serve others with those hands and feet.

Not only did they immobilize Him, they mocked Him, telling Him to "perform another miracle" and come down from the cross. Though Christ had power to perform any miracle, He suffered and listened to them. This is the crucified life. We each must live such a life daily. When we do so, we carry on His work, enabling Jesus to walk and touch through many hands and feet. "When God the Father, with glorious power, brought him back to life again, you were given his wonderful new life to enjoy" (Romans 6:4).

Christ's hands and feet didn't remain nailed. He lives inside the born-again believer, and He therefore has great potential. The Spirit of God gives us spiritual gifts and power. The Bible talks about understanding "how incredibly great his power is to help [us]" (Ephesians 1:19).

As a parent, I have seen how children reflect what they learn and inherit from their parents and environment. It is clear that we all inherit from our parents abilities and talents and character and behavior. Likewise, when Christ comes to live within us, He begins to transform us. He is, even now, changing us from what we are by nature to what we need to be by the will of God. God wants us to bear His character. God wants to work through us. So God gives us character as well as abilities.

This means that veiled character traits must be removed and replaced with good qualities. Our inability to love God and love man must be replaced with ability and strength to do so. Due to our learning and environment, we each have instincts for various actions. Some of these are good, some are bad. We know which areas in our lives need cleansing, and which require further development.

When we allow Christ to come into our lives, we become a combination of genes and training plus what God gives us as a result of accepting Christ. In the mystery of God's grace, all these—heredity, genes, environment, training, and the spiritual components—work together! The spiritual blessings God bestows on me work in harmony with what good qualities God gave me in my genes, environment, and training.

If I disregard the spiritual component, I lose a great deal and become deficient. In the following chapters, I will share more experiences that will help you better see and understand the myriad problems and disadvantages man faces due to this deficiency. And the myriad ways God works to bring about His will and work, despite our deficiencies.

4

Do Not Be
Worried and Upset

GOD IS MUCH BIGGER THAN OUR PROBLEMS

Like most people who travel often, I usually allow myself plenty of time to get to the airport. I also try to take special precautions when I check in for a full flight to ensure I don't lose my seat—and possibly the price of my ticket—if I happen to be late. When there are a lot of people traveling, it can be difficult to get a seat on subsequent flights. Also, taking a flight other than the one you originally booked can be both inconvenient and risky—luggage, connecting flights, meeting people, all of these factors become a cause for anxiety. So, as you can imagine, people such as I who travel often generally do all we can do to make our planned flights. However, "all we can do" sometimes isn't good enough.

On one trip in India I sat next to a passenger who had been given the window seat. When the flight attendant came around with beverages, she poured tea for us. She had to lean over my tray table, as the passenger sitting in the window seat was reluctant to lift his cup for her to pour into it. During the process she spilled some tea on his tray table. Immediately I took my paper napkin and offered to wipe down the tray table, but he refused.

Instead, he began to spill more tea from his cup on the tray and then folded the tray so that the back of the seat in front of him got soaked with tea! He also made sure the materials in the seat pocket in front of him got wet before the attendant returned with more paper napkins. I began to wonder if I would be his next target when the flight attendant collected the tray and cup, apologizing for the spill. As she walked away, I glanced at my seatmate, wondering why in the world he was behaving so strangely.

"I think we're on time today," I said, trying to break the ice.

"What's the use?" he responded.

"Are you going to be late for your next appointment, sir?" I asked politely.

"I was supposed to leave yesterday," he said with a coarse, angry voice. "But those wretched airline people gave my seat to someone else."

"I'm so sorry to hear that!" I said with sympathy, and he went on to tell me that because his car had broken down on the way to the airport, he hadn't arrived in time for check-in. Since there were a lot of passengers on the waiting list, his seat had been given away after his name had been announced repeatedly over the public address system—which, of course, he could not hear because he was stranded on the highway! When he finally made it to the airport, his flight was closed and all the passengers had passed through the security area.

"I pleaded for my seat," he told me in a pathetic tone, "but they said I couldn't go." It seems he argued a long time with the agents at the check-in counter and exchanged quite a few angry words. He was still angry at the airline staff.

"Did you sleep well last night, sir?" I inquired. He told me he had been promised a seat on the flight the following day, but he'd had to pay for a room in a hotel to spend the night.

"All night I was thinking of the behavior of the airline staff," he explained. "They were very rude to me. They could have given me my seat."

I asked about his occupation and was surprised to learn that he was a qualified surgeon and a member of the Fellowship of the Royal College of Surgeons (F.R.C.S.). Why would such a man react as he had? After all, flight delays and sudden flight cancellations are not uncommon in India.

I wondered how he would respond when something went wrong in the operation theater; it was frightening to think of his holding the surgical knife while behaving as he did in the airplane. Sometimes even highly educated people behave like beasts, especially when they are angry about unpredictable happenings.

I smiled at him and said, "Things that are out of our control are on the increase, aren't they?" I told him how, when tap water became available in my home village, we all buried our wells and now depend entirely on tap water. If something goes wrong with the water works department, including electrical failure, we don't have water from the tap. In the past, water had been under our direct control. Now, thanks to modern technology, it wasn't.

"Although I am not in control, my great big, wonderful God is," I continued. "For instance, I may be about to solve some pressing problems when another heap of problems suddenly come up." He looked at me and encouraged me to continue.

"But my great big, wonderful God is much much bigger than all my problems put together!" As I talked to the man, he began to share his personal problems in response. I went on to tell him that though we know that our God is sovereign and in full control, we often try to make our problems bigger and our God smaller. This is foolishness, plain and simple. I explained how one can find rest and peace in God's power and care.

"These concepts will help me in my work," he responded. He did not have much difficulty in accepting God and spiritual reality and the methods and procedures based on faith—even atheists have endorsed the faith method.

For example, one atheist told me a story about a rich father who handed over the keys of his possessions to his only son. He told his son about one small room in their big house and showed him the key to that room. He wanted his son to know what was so special about that room. The father explained that the small room was full of gold plates kept for the welfare of future generations. He gave his son the key on one condition: that the son should not open that room unless it was essential. Otherwise, the son was to make his way on his own.

The son never needed to open the room. His business thrived despite the many risks he took. After accumulating a lot of wealth, however, the son wanted to look at the gold plates in the small room. But when he turned the key and opened the door, he found nothing but an empty room. There was no sign of any gold plates! The moral of this story is that even if an all-powerful God doesn't exist, it is better to assume that He does and take all the risks victoriously.

The surgeon I met on the plane, however, did not want to assume things like that. Instead, he decided to subject his new-found beliefs to the test of experience. His practice is going wonderfully now, and he reports he is a different person. He does not become so upset over things that come up unexpectedly. He has discovered, as we all can discover, that if Christ is living in you, you are being transformed every day.

Is it necessary to get upset and worried? Not at all. We can know God is in control. This is not a mere assumption on our parts. Day by day, we experience God's control on us. Most of us know the story of the young boy who was flying a kite. He used a long string, and the kite flew so high that he had to look very carefully to locate it in the sky. One elderly uncle came to the boy and mocked him for looking at the sky and holding on to a string. The uncle was not convinced that the kite was flying in the sky. All the boy could tell him was to feel the tension on the string!

We live by faith, but it is with adequate evidence of what is not seen. We can experiment and prove the reality of God in our lives. Because of this, our faith is totally different from the story of the gold plates. We are not like the son who believes in something that is not there. When we open the door to our special room, it will hold the greatest treasure of all: a holy and all-powerful God!

BLESS OTHERS AS YOU ARE BEING BLESSED

We must do our best to protect ourselves from any negative happenings. But we need not be overly concerned. Instead, we need to learn to relax in the sovereignty of God.

I thought I did everything right when I planned a short trip to an evening meeting. I checked the car, started it, and even examined the engine. Satisfied the car was ready, I went inside for a brief time of prayer. But when I went back to the car, it wouldn't start. I tried for a few minutes, but it was getting late.

Finally, I had to call a taxi. When it finally arrived, I discovered that the driver was new to the area. He had just recently started his taxi business after a stint in the army.

Because he was unfamiliar with the roads, he had an assistant with him. As he drove out onto the main road, I thought: *Even a bullock cart can overtake our taxi. He came late and now he goes slow. It's already time for my speech!* I was tempted to get out of that cab and hire another.

But all I said to the taxi driver was, "Who knows, the one person who is going to listen to my speech may not arrive until we get there." He looked at me confused, so I went on to explain. "I am going to this place just for one person, the one person who needs to hear what I have to say and who needs to know my God. He might be working late somewhere and get to the meeting only by the time I get there."

I encouraged him not to speed just because I was in a hurry. He seemed to relax, and I asked him to tell me about his new business. He told me his plans for settling his children, renovating his old house, and taking care of other personal matters. Then, finally, we reached the meeting place—almost an hour late.

I asked the driver to stay for my return trip and then straightway went to the stage. Once there I found that some of the young people had been singing all the songs they knew to keep the audience entertained as they waited for me to arrive. I spoke for about forty-five minutes and went back to the taxi for the return trip home. As we drove toward the main road, the driver asked me who that "one person" was, the person I had mentioned on my way to the meeting. I told him it must have been someone in the crowd.

"I am that one person," the taxi driver said in a loud voice. "I had the privilege of entering the kingdom of God tonight."

"There were two persons who entered the kingdom of God tonight," his assistant said with a soft voice. "I am the second person." I told the driver to pull over and park on the side of the road for a moment. I wanted them to tell me what they understood from the message I had given from the platform.

"We were listening to you while you were in the taxi," one of them said. The other one nodded agreement. It seems they had been observing my reaction to the delay and listening to my tone of voice as we talked. I'd had every reason to be upset, but God had enabled me to talk to them and encourage them even though we were late.

The two men in the taxi had decided to listen to me speak, and in the course of my talk they met the same Jesus who lives in me. I explained to them the qualities of Christ and the way they can have His new life. I told them how Christ could improve each of them in their character and give them power to react in more positive, encouraging ways.

Someone once said: "It is better to light a candle in a dark room rather than to curse the darkness." Our small light can shine out for others. I am not perfect, but those men were able to find Christ who *is* perfect. The living Christ activates us spiritually, and I was happy that those men were activated by Christ.

I have had many occasions when I was on my way to deliver a message, and I will have many more. Each time is an opportunity. I can choose to spend my traveling time thinking of my problems, such as car troubles, train delays, certain words others used against me, etc. But how can I listen to God's voice when I am preoccupied with all these cares and worries? I am unnecessarily causing myself stress. It is better to go straight to the One who said: "Come to me and I will give you rest—all of you who work so hard beneath a heavy yoke" (Matthew 11:28). If you replace the worry-producing thoughts with good and valuable thoughts, you will benefit physically as well. The Bible says: "Fix your thoughts on what is true and good and right. Think about things that are pure and lovely, and dwell on the fine, good things in others. Think about all you can praise God for and be glad about" (Philippians 4:8).

PUT CHARACTER BEFORE WORK

In communication classes I have learned that "the medium is the message." God gave us the greatest message wrapped up in the person of Christ. When we have Christ in us, we also have God's message in us. So when envy, jealousy, and bitterness are seen in our lives, people cannot help but wonder what kind of Christ lives in us. If we wish to be true examples of Christ, we must work on a daily basis to improve our character.

I remember how I looked once when I had been sick for two weeks. It felt so good to shave! Since I hadn't done so for two weeks, I found a different face looking back at me in the mirror after I'd gotten cleaned up. I looked different to myself and others.

Similarly, I must be different in my attitude and behavior every day. We are set apart for such improvement in our character. From the very beginning God decided that we should become like Jesus (see Romans 8:29). Our hatred must be replaced with love, our anxiety with peace, our bitterness with forgiveness. Even when things seem to be going against us, God can make this work for us and for our benefit. We may not know how such things as a flight delay or a transportation problem or a loss of property will work in our favor, but God does. He is using all of our failures, worries, sickness, pain, painful experiences, victories, peace of mind, healing of sickness, financial gain—He is using everything to help me become more like Christ.

We just have to trust God. Our worry shows a lack of trust in God. These days many people invite various kinds of physical illnesses by worrying and getting upset. When we focus on negative experiences and there seem to be no peaceful and joyful experiences to compensate, the stress can affect us psychologically and physically. That is why we need to smile even at the storm.

These days people talk about "smilage" to explain how your smile keeps you physically fit. How can you keep smiling even in adverse situations? Consider the early disciples. They were beaten and denied their rights, yet they were found rejoicing (see Acts 5:41). When you have the assurance of your future in Christ, you can be courageous and joyful. God has already decided to take care of you. When we travel by air, we take our seats and trust the pilot. When we travel by faith, even though there may be storms ahead, we know that our Pilot is with us, and He is able to negotiate any turbulence we may face.

You may be responsible for many important and urgent matters. If so, it's easy to become upset over a five-minute flight delay. But always remember that our God can work out any situation. Ultimately, as we learn to rely on and rest in Him, we learn that there is no need—or benefit—to being worried and hurried.

One key to learning this is recognizing that God is more interested in our faithful obedience than in our success at any cost. If our focus is moved from what God wants done to what we want done, we will have all sorts of unnecessary worries. God's work is being done through us; all we need to do is our best and leave the results to God. God will be glorified through us, and the work will be done.

Of course, it isn't always easy to keep that in mind. Too often we get caught up in what we are doing. Our outward activities are important, but we must take care of our inner man first. And we need to check whether we are doing a lot of things to cover up the fact that we have neglected our inner man. Let Christ into the inner areas of your life. He is waiting to clean up those areas and strengthen you. The Holy Spirit is ready to transform you, helping you to keep your will in line with God's will.

Someone has said: "The safest place to be is within the will of God." But it is only through the Spirit's intervention that we can be there, in God's will. When we try to control our lives independently of God, we end up in a mess because "we naturally love to do evil things that are just the opposite of the things that the Holy Spirit tells us to do; and the good things we want to do when the Spirit has his way with us are just the opposite of our natural desires. These two forces within us are constantly fighting each other to win control over us, and our wishes are never free from their pressures" (Galatians 5:17).

God wants His will to be accomplished in our lives. And He is ready to help us follow the good things of the Spirit. "If we are living now by the Holy Spirit's power, let us follow the Holy Spirit's leading in every part of our lives" (Galatians 5:25). Once again, we can be secure in the fact that we do not face life alone. We have an Almighty God who will go through everything with us, strengthening us and guiding us in His ways.

5

Go Beyond
the Material
and Technology

A FAITH EVEN SCIENTISTS HAVE TO BELIEVE

I don't find it difficult to believe in God. As a scientist, I often have to exercise faith. Any time I do research, I have to believe that what I am exploring, such as nature, is real. It would be difficult to explore something that is unreal or only appears to be real. I don't know all there is to know about nature. But I can build on what I do know—that nature does exist. Therefore, when I begin to explore something, to research it, I demonstrate my faith in that thing's existence. Similarly, when I pray I show that I believe in God's existence.

As a scientist, I also have to believe in the regularity of events in nature. I may have to wait until next year to find whether certain things will operate the same way as they did this year. But until I am shown differently, I go ahead with my research, believing that nature is unchanging.

Similarly, I can boldly believe the unchanging promises of God. God will care for me, God will be close beside me, and God will provide for me (sometimes, but not always, even bypassing the laws of nature!). God's promises are unchanging because God is unchanging. In Him are wisdom, power, holiness, goodness, justice, and truth. That will never change.

As a scientist, I explore nature believing that it is understandable. There is no point in working hard if nature is not understandable. Then, as I continue exploring, I am able to unravel the mysteries of nature. Likewise, though God is infinite and I am finite, I believe that He is understandable to the extent that He reveals Himself through Christ and in His Word. So I can begin my exploration believing that I will, at least in part, be able to understand God.

When I first began my work as a scientist, I had to study systematically, intelligently, and diligently. I would start with the accumulated knowledge that others had discovered regarding my topic of study. I had to learn how they obtained proof and what methodology they adopted. As a person who wants to know God, I can adopt the same methodology in studying the Scriptures, which contain a record of what others, by divine inspiration, have written about God.

I have carried out experiments with the help of experienced scientists to prove my personal convictions. I also have had to rely on the experiments conducted by others. Experiencing the living presence and abiding love of God in my life can be verified on an experimental basis. In fact, God is verifying Himself to us through various life experiences. There is a difference between the understanding of a person who has experienced the living presence of God and the one who has not yet experienced it.

To understand that difference, consider Matthew 5:8: "Happy are those whose hearts are pure, for they shall see God." In science we wouldn't say that only the pure in heart can see, say, a nuclear reactor. Anyone, pure or impure, can see a nuclear reactor. But in Scripture, what is real for the pure in heart more than likely won't be real for the impure. What is true and real for the person who has experienced the living presence of God likely won't be true and real for the one who has not yet experienced Him.

In science, we continue to carry on independent investigations to unravel greater mysteries of nature. As we gain more information, we publish it for the benefit of others. Similarly, when we have other kinds of experiences—especially experiences of a spiritual nature—we should share what we learn for the benefit of others.

In the following chapters, I will recount more of my spiritual experiences to share with you what I am learning, day by day, and how I find courage in a world of discouragement.

Putting Your Life on the Line

There is one thing I have discovered as a scientist: Technology is wonderful! It is an integral part of our lives today. Often we use and rely on technology without even being aware of it. Sometimes, we even put our lives on the line for it. This was brought to my attention one morning as I was having breakfast in my hotel room. The hotel receptionist phoned me to let me know there was a man waiting for me in the lobby.

I did not expect anyone that morning since my host already had made all arrangements for my ride to the airport. The telephone operator arranged for me to speak to the unexpected visitor over the in-house telephone.

"I came to thank you for your help," he told me in a grateful voice.

"What for?" I was curious.

"For saving my life!" he said, surprising me. "I was in

your audience last night. I thought you were talking about my condition in your speech. Thank you for helping me!"

Now I was even more curious! When he asked me to pray with him, I invited him to come up to my room.

While I waited for him, I thought over the previous night. I had spoken at a dinner meeting arranged by some friends who are interested in spiritual things. They had invited some of their colleagues, and they had asked me to speak to the group.

I had talked about our relationship with God. I explained how our other relationships are affected due to damage caused by sin. I discussed the fact that, originally, man was made in the image of God. But due to man's sin, his image was defaced. Of course, the good news is that our defaced images can be restored in Jesus Christ. And when our relationship with God is restored, our relationship with others in the sociological dimension, with ourselves in the psychological dimension, and even with our environment in the ecological dimension can all be improved. And we can prove this restoration by subjecting our beliefs to the test of experience.

When my visitor arrived, I showed him to a seat. He began talking immediately: "Several times I have thought of attempting suicide, but then I thought of others and that prevented me from doing it." He went on to describe his strained relationships at home and at work.

He told me he reached the point where he couldn't even stand the sight of other people talking when he was around them because he always assumed they were talking about him. He said he almost became psychotic. He did not want to live and was waiting for an opportunity to take his life. This was disturbing to begin with, but it became even more so when he informed me that he was a commercial airline pilot. He hinted that he had even attempted suicide.

"Then," he said, a smile lighting up his face, "I heard you speak. And now everything has changed! I do not want to die; I only want to live. And I know God will help me to do so, and He will help restore me and my relationships."

After we prayed together and he left, I began to think of people like this man in whose hands we place our lives and safety. I was grateful that God had used me to help this man. And God helped me see that when we open ourselves to be used by Him, we may well be helping many other people too—such as those who could have been passengers in an airplane being flown by a troubled and suicidal person.

God knows how much we depend on technology in our world. But even more, He knows that there is an element we often overlook: the human element. And when that element is in trouble, we become the tools through which God works His loving, healing will.

MAN NEEDS MORE THAN MEDICINE

Negative emotions are everywhere. We grow angry, feel insulted, and begin to resent. Slowly but surely, grudges build in our hearts and minds. It requires a tremendous amount of emotional energy to keep a grudge going. When we nurse and hold onto grudges, we let bitterness grow within us. And bitterness is like a poison that can affect us physically, mentally, and spiritually.

Another powerful negative emotion is guilt. When guilt over what we've done threatens to overwhelm us, we need to do something to gain a clear conscience. The apostle Paul stated: "I try with all my strength to always maintain a clear conscience before God and man" (Acts 24:16).

The airline pilot who visited me that morning at my

hotel had discovered the joy of a cleansed conscience. During our visit, he told me how that very day he had called the people with whom he had a strained relationship and asked them to forgive him. The reason he was able to do this was that at the dinner meeting where he'd heard me speak, he had asked God for the strength to "crucify his pride."

Pride is a big hindrance to getting a clear conscience. Our pride always tells us we are right and others are wrong. But that seldom is the case. Whenever we are wrong, whether in our actions or attitudes, we need to admit that before God.

The first step to admitting we are wrong is to identify our basic offense. Sometimes we belittle people. We may not recognize their value and worth. We may have no concern for other people and their welfare. We may even be party to the exploitation and oppression of the weak. Or we may be guilty of hatred, ungratefulness, resentment, and so forth.

Whatever our wrong is, we need to ask forgiveness. "If we confess our sins to him, he can be depended on to forgive us and to cleanse us from every wrong. [And it is perfectly proper for God to do this for us because Christ died to wash away our sins.]" (1 John 1:9). Whatever we have done against God, we have to settle with God. He is, in fact, waiting for you to approach Him. Whatever wrongs we have committed against people, we have to ask that person or persons to forgive us. If we have caused any material or similar damage, we have to make restitution for the same.

I realize this sounds frightening or difficult. But it is necessary for cleansing your conscience. Sometimes you may have to prepare yourself beforehand to make sure what you are going to say. We read in the story of the prodigal son that the young man decided first in his heart what he would tell his father: "I will go home to my father and say, 'Father, I have sinned against both heaven and you, and am no longer worthy of being called your son'" (Luke 15:18–19). Later on, we read that he used exactly the same wording (see Luke 15:21) when he approached his father.

It is important, though, to realize that while God will readily forgive us, people may not be so inclined. There may be someone who will not forgive you. If this happens, don't worry; simply concentrate on sincerely and prayerfully doing your part. Leave the rest to the One who can heal all wounds, and melt all hearts. The end result is in God's hands, not ours. We need only do our part and leave the rest to Him.

GET RID OF BITTERNESS

Holding feelings of hurt and bitterness also affects our spiritual and physical health. The Bible says:

"Stop being mean, bad-tempered and angry. Quarreling, harsh words, and dislike of others should have no place in your lives. Instead, be kind to each other, tenderhearted, forgiving one another, just as God has forgiven you because you belong to Christ" (Ephesians 4:31–32).

How can we forgive people? When others do things against us, it is natural to feel offended. And we often blame the offender for the problem. But the more we blame them, the more we build anger and dislike against others. Before we know it, we get worked up inside and waste a lot of time and energy.

Our body chemistry often gets upset in that agitated condition, and we become prone to certain kinds of sicknesses. We unnecessarily invite physical illnesses when we give in to wrong responses to unpleasant situations. Our muscle, nerve, and body systems are affected. What a price to pay for anger and bitterness!

As Christians, we know that God watches over the affairs of His children. Nothing happens to us that He doesn't know about or that is out of His control. So what does this mean when we feel offended? Should we suppress our negative feelings when someone wrongs us? *No.* If you suppress such things, they will just build up until they explode someday. Instead, we can try to understand what is happening.

When someone has wronged you, try to find out whether you have somehow contributed to the problem. If you discover that you are somehow in the wrong too, do your best to rectify the situation. However, there will be times when people wrong you without any provocation or contribution on your part. You may be fully innocent and the other person may be fully wrong. So how do you forgive someone in that situation?

One tool that may help you to forgive is to view the offender differently. When we are up in a plane, even skyscrapers look like "match boxes." The buildings are still tall, but they look small because our perspective is changed. When someone has wronged you, especially when that person is 100 percent wrong, you have every reason to feel resentment. But what good will holding anger and bitterness do you? Such wrong responses only add to the problem, and could possibly cause you emotional or physical stress. Ultimately, you become the loser.

Sometimes you can fight something out until you feel you have "won." But that may be of little use if you end up sick because of the stress and intensity of the process. Instead, try changing your perspective. Trusting God, you can boldly say that whatever anyone has done against you will be to your own advantage in the long run. In this way, you can consider the wrongdoer to be a tool in God's hand. Just see the person as someone being used by God to bring blessings to you, even though the offender's aim may have been to destroy you. If you believe that you are ultimately going to be blessed through the offender's actions, you can praise God for him. Then there is no need to hold anger or bitterness.

With God's help, you can turn your bitterness into forgiveness. You can stop being mean, bad-tempered, and angry. You may not know what good is going to happen to you as a result of someone's wrongdoings, but you can learn to avoid hurting yourself by holding on to negative responses. You can learn how to forgive from the bottom of your heart, how to love the offender, and even how to show the one who has wronged you some kindness.

When we open ourselves to God's love and let Him control our reactions, His love takes over and expels hurt feelings. When we forgive, we feel the burden is gone; and, instead of thinking about the offender all the time, we can use our time better. Time is so precious. Some think that they have millions of minutes, and so they waste time. What we fill our time with is actually very important. When we constantly think of those we don't like, we keep living through their actions and so get irritated inside. This can become so distracting that it hinders our concentration and work, making us prone to carelessness and errors. It also can exhaust us physically and mentally.

God has forgiven us on the basis of what Jesus accomplished on the cross. We can first receive forgiveness for our own wrong responses and then forgive others. You may need to turn to God to cleanse your heart and obtain forgiveness. But you don't need to go to anyone to forgive others; you can do it yourself right now. Thank God for forgiving you and then simply forgive others from your heart.

We read in the Bible that "If you want to keep from becoming fainthearted and weary, think about [Jesus'] patience as sinful men did such terrible things to him" (Hebrews 12:3). Yes, sinful men did terrible things to Jesus, but He was patient in all things. This means that instead of thinking about the evil character traits of offenders, we are asked to think about the qualities of Jesus. If we focus on patience, kindness, goodness and love, we will be able to acquire those qualities of Jesus. The more we meditate on and copy these good qualities in place of the wrong and opposite ones, the more we become like Jesus.

It is better, then, to get rid of bitterness and resentment and replace them with Christlike behavior. God has designed us to shift our focus to Jesus and His qualities instead of concentrating on the offenders. We are destined to possess those good qualities. If we are inviting deterioration on the inside by our wrong responses, it is time to shift and "fix your thoughts on what is true and good and right. Think about things that are pure and lovely, and dwell on the fine, good things in others" (Philippians 4:8).

6

Turning the Worst Into the Best

I Have My Rights . . . or Do I?

"I've got my rights!" We've all said something similar to this at one time or another in our lives. Having rights is important to us. It means we're someone who deserves consideration and respect, who deserves to be acknowledged and listened to. We feel discontented and angry when we think we've been denied our rights—especially when the situation happens unexpectedly. I had to go through such an experience during one of my trips a few years ago.

I normally look for the least expensive tourist ticket, thereby being a better steward of money. Often such tourist tickets are restricted to a single airline all throughout the trip. If I miss a particular flight on that airline, I have to wait till the next available flight.

For this particular trip, I was to depart on a Tuesday morning from the international airport and continue with connections all the way to Los Angeles, where I was to attend meetings Wednesday through Friday. I was to leave soon after the meetings on Friday night to get back home for some other programs. The entire trip would be canceled if I was unable to make it to the international airport on time that Tuesday morning.

To arrive on time, I reserved a seat well in advance on a domestic flight that would get me to where I needed to be the night before departure. The domestic flight took off on time Monday evening, but it was diverted to another airport due to some problem. We all realized that there was no way to get to the international airport because of this diversion—especially when we heard the announcement that we would have to remain overnight at the diversion area.

As usual, the ground staff distributed complimentary hotel vouchers for the night stay to all the stranded passengers, but there was no ground transportation available. We were advised to take taxis in groups according to the hotels assigned to us. Because of the increasing demand and the lack of taxicabs at that time of night, we had to wait for a long time before a taxi was available for our group.

Finally, my turn came—or so I thought. I had two pieces of luggage while others in our group only had hand-carried bags. As I was about to load my suitcase, a stout man in the group pushed me out and allowed his friend who was not in line to get in, and so the taxi left without me.

As we were all strangers to one another and everyone wanted to get some sleep in the hotel, no one bothered to interfere when my right to board the taxi was violated. I didn't make any noise about it either. I quietly carried my luggage back to the very end of the taxi line, saying "Praise the Lord" in my heart as I was walking back.

"Praise the Lord," I said again, a little more loudly this time, since we are asked to thank and praise the Lord for all things at all times (see Colossians 1:12; Ephesians 5:20). So there we stood, waiting for the taxis that only occasionally showed up. By now it was getting very late at night. Suddenly I noticed a private car stopping near the line, and a man got out to search for someone. This gentleman came to the end of the line and started talking to the two passengers behind me. Earlier, when I realized those two had been given vouchers to stay in the same hotel to which I was assigned, I had asked them to join me for the taxi ride since it could seat four people.

As I listened to the conversation they had with the visitor who had come looking for them, I realized that one of them was the chief manager of a firm and that the visitor was his junior manager in that city. During a telephone conversation, he had come to know that his superior manager was stranded at this domestic airport. I saw the two passengers getting ready to go with the visitor in his car. I wished I could go with them since they were going to my hotel. At that time of the night it would also be much safer to ride with someone in a private car rather than in a taxi.

Just when I resigned myself to continuing my wait for the taxi, the men looked at me and invited me to join them. I continued praising the Lord in my heart while I moved toward the private car with those kind men. I loaded my suitcase in the trunk; and after we all got seated comfortably, we proceeded to the hotel. I thanked the Lord for the man who had crowded into the line a few minutes earlier. I thanked and praised the Lord for the ride and the company of those men. The chief manager suggested that we have dinner together before going to our rooms.

At dinner, I thought again about the fact that I would not be able to reach the international airport in time the next morning, and so I would have to cancel my trip. The next available flight would be on Friday, and my meeting in Los Angeles would be over then. That meant there was no point in continuing with this stranded flight since practically all hope of reaching the international airport was very dim.

During our conversation at the dinner table, the chief manager expressed the importance of his reaching the international airport at least by early morning. I also expressed my need to be there early to make my intended flight. I told them I had decided to go back home if I could not reach the international airport the next morning.

The junior manager immediately offered his car, filled with gas, and a driver to drive all night. After dinner we all got back into the car and drove through the night. In the morning, when we arrived at the international airport, they dropped me off right on time at the departure area!

Why did I say "Praise the Lord" for that stout man's pushing me out of line and for being denied my rights? I knew God was in charge, and that we must praise God at all times for all things. As it turned out, God used this man and his "offense" to work things out for me, to ensure that I would not miss the best. If I had gone in the taxi, I would have slept in that hotel and returned home the next day.

God had wanted me to attend the meetings, and He knew I was standing in line with the wrong group. God wanted to separate me from that group. I would not have left that group on my own since it was natural and logical to stay with them and proceed to the hotel. God knew this, and so He allowed someone to "wrong" me that I might be blessed with His abundance and supply.

Why should I get upset over a simple denial of my rights when I believe in a God who is so interested in my welfare? I may try to reason and argue my case, but finally I will come back to my limitations—and God's ultimate control. When we praise God during frustrating or difficult times, we are actually thanking and praising God for taking care of us and doing the best for us. In so doing, you can defeat your depressions and disappointments, and be set free from bitterness. Enjoying peace in such situations is advantageous to your physical as well as your mental health. God does step in to help you. You can trust Him, even in the midst of an undesirable situation. You do not need to worry even if all your plans are upset through undesirable events. God is in control.

Of course, saying "Praise God" is not a magic formula. You will encounter some difficulties that will not seem to work out "to your best." But even if our difficulties amount to suffering and inconvenience, we know that God will be with us as we go through them. God has promised us his presence at all times. "I am holding you by your right hand—I, the Lord your God—and I say to you, Don't be afraid; I am here to help you" (Isaiah 41:13). God has promised us His abiding presence, "that I am with you always, even to the end of the world" (Matthew 28:20). Why should I get upset when God is close beside me? "Even when walking through the dark valley of death I will not be afraid, for you are close beside me, guarding, guiding all the way" (Psalm 23:4).

You are not suppressing your anger and resentment by praising God. You do not have to deny that you are hurt or upset. The more you pretend on the outside, the more harm it does within you. The anger and feelings of hurt will build, and you may end up taking things out on people who aren't even involved—your family, employees, etc. Don't deny or suppress your feelings. Acknowledge them to your loving Father, then let them go. And simply begin to look at events and the people with a different attitude: "I don't like what has happened, but I know Who is in control. And I trust Him to work His will in this situation."

Be assured, God can turn even the worst things into the best. "And we know that all that happens to us is working for our good if we love God and are fitting into his plans" (Romans 8:28). Your trust in Him will not be in vain.

He will be there for you.

Are You Willing to Give Up?

Like it or not, we must be willing to give up our rights. It may be legitimate to possess certain items, hold certain positions, aspire for certain benefits, etc. But we must be willing to give up our rights for Jesus' sake, even as He gave up His rights when He became a man (see Philippians 2:6–7).

We can follow the pattern Jesus showed us in yielding our rights to God. We are not our own; we are under God's mercy. All that belongs to us was given to us. We are stewards of all that is in our possession, including our good environment, training and health. There is nothing wrong, therefore, in yielding our rights to God. Most quarrels deal with someone violating someone else's rights. If we hold onto our rights too tightly, we will be creating more tension and subsequent quarrels.

Consider a typical home and family. The father, mother, children, and others in the household will all have some personal rights. If each one of them holds tightly to his or her rights, there is bound to be some violation. And the result will be quarrels, misunderstandings, and disturbance of the family atmosphere. There will be more enemies in the family than loved ones! But if the members of the family are willing to give up their personal rights, they can then afford to be flexible and open to compromise.

The bottom line is this: we really do not lose anything when we surrender our rights to God. We read in the Bible how Abraham went through this experience when he laid his beloved son, Isaac, on the altar. Abraham had every right to argue his case when he was asked to perform such a painful task. It is very difficult to place something you really love on the altar of sacrifice. There will be a lot of struggle in your mind whether what you are doing is right and proper. But we know that in the case of Abraham, he trusted God fully.

When we yield our rights, fully trusting, we can relax over what feels like a loss. God is interested in meeting our needs, and so there is no need to worry. In the case of Abraham, God gave Isaac back to him with greater blessings (see Genesis 22:10–12). Likewise, God gives us back a lot of privileges when we yield our rights to Him. As we live without any rights, there is no fear of anyone's violating our rights. If someone infringes on our rights at all, we are not even in the picture. The rights given to God are violated, and so God will take care of His property. When we have no rights remaining to be violated, there is no need to become angry. Once you transfer your rights and ownership to God, you can really relax.

Dealing with being denied our rights is hard enough when it is "accidental" or just a circumstantial event. But what about situations in which people cheat you knowingly? Well, when the Scriptures tell us "all that happens" works together for good, cheating is included also.

I remember a time when I was cheated out of one hundred rupees ($7.00). The amount of money involved was small, but the money wasn't really the issue. What troubled me was that I had been cheated by someone whom I would never have expected to cheat me. *He should not have done that to me,* I said to myself. At that point, I had two choices. I could let my hurt feelings build, get worked up inside, and eventually develop hatred, bitterness, and resentment. Or I could admit my hurt, then let it go and say in my heart that the person who cheated me had only done something good to me. I could view his actions as something done in my favor, regardless of the man's intent.

We may be shocked by people's actions at times. At such times, it is helpful to see these people in light of the good things God is going to bring to our lives. In certain cases we see the positive result quickly; in other cases, much later. We may not even see the benefit for a long time. But God will definitely work it out for our advantage.

In this case, it did not take many years to see the result of the cheating. I learned that I gained eight thousand four hundred rupees ($588)! If I hadn't been cheated three months earlier, I would have lost that much money. You may well be amazed at the ways God works in what seems to be a loss to bring you abundant blessing! And His blessings go far beyond material wealth. He wants us to have the blessings of character, because we are predestined to become like Jesus (see Romans 8:29). This means that we receive the qualities of Jesus. Such qualities in life are more valuable than thousands of rupees. So, look for the Christlike qualities God will form in you as a result of going through difficult times. As you change your perspective about the things that happen to you, you will find God bringing you both spiritual and physical blessings.

Give Up Your Rights—And Enjoy!

If you still get upset when you see someone violating the rights you once owned, it means you have not yet yielded your rights. You only said you did. God gives to us according to our need. But when God gives things to us, we need to remember that the gifts He gives are not given as rights, but as privileges to enjoy.

Assume that you gave up your rights to three hundred dollars, or three hundred acres of land, or anything substantial. When you give up your rights on that three hundred whatever, God may give you back two hundred—not as rights, but as privileges to meet your need. God knows that your exact need is two hundred and so He gives back that.

Sometimes God knows that three hundred is much smaller than your need. In such cases, God may give back not the three hundred you gave up, but ten thousand. Don't waste your time and energy struggling and quarreling over what you think you deserve. Trust God, who may take away your three hundred so that He can give you ten thousand to meet your exact need.

It is always better to yield your rights to God and enjoy His provision. God knows how to handle what is given to Him, even when it seems He and you are being cheated. God can turn the worst cheating into something that is wonderful. God has sufficient resources to use every form of violation for your good. But first you have to trust God and His provisions and sufficiency.

However, we need to remember that though our rights are yielded, our responsibilities are not. We must faithfully obey God in discharging our duties and responsibilities. God supplies us with the power to carry on; we supply Him with our willingness to do our best and keep trusting.

We know that we will have problems as long as we live in this world. We face tense situations, especially when we have to do several things at the same time. In a string instrument, there will be good music when the strings are stretched properly. If there is no tension in the string, the instrument cannot produce good music. If there is too much tension, the string is likely to break. We should not allow tension to break us physically, mentally, or spiritually. But we must feel the tension and pain to deal with situations in life.

A friend once told me a story about a bridge that was being built. The engineer who designed the bridge knew the maximum load allowable. He knew what materials had to be used and how they had to be constructed to be sure the bridge was safe and serviceable. Similarly, we can be sure that the "Heavenly Engineer" knows our maximum tension and suffering. Difficulties will not crush us. "When you go through deep waters and great trouble, I will be with you. When you go through rivers of difficulty, you will not drown! When you walk through the fire of oppression, you will not be burned up—the flames will not consume you" (Isaiah 43:2).

We regularly face difficulties and oppression. Those fearful things are not going to harm us. God is in control! We should not let fear and disappointments defeat us. We have all the resources available in Christ. We can truly praise God for all things at all times.

7

Expectations and "The God Factor"

FINDING THE PERFECT MAN (OR WOMAN)

Are arranged marriages out of fashion? It seems that the pressures from parents and dowry deaths* are quoted to discredit all arranged marriages. Those who counsel young couples are able to give a lot of data on incompatibility, interpersonal difficulties, mother-in-law problems, etc., of both arranged and for-love marriages. Is there a foolproof method of selecting your life partner? Or do you hand everything over to chance, horoscopes, immediate advantages, and the like?

In the tradition in which I grew up, the parents arrange the marriages of their children. In fact, the parents and uncles and aunts and other close relatives conduct some research about the family and the background of a prospective mate. They look for and ensure that the positive factors outweigh the negative.

Hearing that a person belongs to a family of reputable people like bishops, professionals, or men of charity makes

* In India, when a daughter is married, her father has to give a dowry (a large sum of money) to the boy's father. If part of the money is not given, for any reason, the daughter's in-laws will harass and persecute her, putting pressure on her to pay. This sometimes results in suicide.

some alliances more attractive. Discoveries of murderers, thieves, divorcees, or mental patients repel the researchers from further inquiry. The present status of the boy, girl, their parents, and advantages of the proposed alliance are considered in most cases. Only when the family members are satisfied will the boy be asked to see the girl who has been chosen as his wife.

I was working in Bombay when my parents were looking for a wife for me. My parents wrote me about the process, and I used to feel nervous when news about some marriage proposal reached me. I knew my entire future would depend on the kind of person I would marry. When I left the matter to God, I began to feel some peace that God would bring only the girl of His choice. However, I was interested in seeing certain abilities in the girl, and so I began to pray that God would bring a girl with all the qualities and abilities on my list.

My list was not very long, but I did want the girl to have at least a degree in science. Since I am a scientist, I felt that was necessary. I also wanted a girl who could sing well, since I am not good at music, and who shared my language and culture. I wanted the girl to be able to help young people spiritually, since I was involved in spiritual ministry among the educated youths. Most importantly, I wanted a girl who was a committed believer.

As I was praying over this list, the Lord asked me whether I was willing to place the list on the altar just like Abraham laid Isaac at God's command. I was confused. What did that mean? Was it wrong for me to desire all these good things in my wife? No, God was not saying that. Rather, He was asking me to be willing to give up my desires, even though they were good! If my high expectations were unmet, I would have felt depressed and worried. God showed me that it is better to leave even the good and legitimate desires on the altar of sacrifice. After much prayer for strength, I placed the list on the altar.

A few days later, word reached me from my parents about a possible wife. I did not know much about her, although I had seen her during a convention so I knew what she looked like. But I had never thought of her becoming my wife. I began to pray about her, asking God to show us if this was the right woman for me. I knew that my parents, and the girl's parents, only wanted the Lord's will to be done in the matter.

After three months of prayer, I felt that perhaps the Lord was leading positively about my marrying this girl. But there is an important custom in our tradition for the man and woman to see each other and give their response to the parents. This is the occasion where we actually know whether something positive is going to evolve. (I knew there were cases where parents imposed their decisions on the man and woman, even though the verdict after the seeing-each-other ceremony was negative. But there was nothing like that to be afraid of in the case of our parents.) If the proposed alliance fails during this ceremony, the parents will continue looking until a suitable mate is found. This means the man will have to see several women, and the women will have to be ready for a chain of appearances until a marriage is finalized.

But when the time came, I could not go to see the woman my parents had chosen. I was in Bombay and was utilizing all my leave for Christian conferences and the like. Moreover, I could not afford to make several trips between Bombay and Kerala. I felt very strongly that this girl was God's gift to me. I did not receive any special revelation, but I began to experience peace over the matter. The question wasn't my feeling, but how I would know whether the girl also felt the same way. I knew I had peace, but what about her? Since I did not have any available leave that year, and I wanted to bypass the seeing ceremony, I did something—with my parents' knowledge—that we normally do not do: I wrote the girl a letter. I addressed her and then wrote these words: "Magnify the Lord with me and let us exalt his Name together . . . and that all things be unto the praise of his glory." I then signed the letter and mailed it.

It only took three days for that letter to reach her. I received the following reply seven days later: "This is the Lord's doing and it is marvelous in our eyes . . . that in all things Christ must have the preeminence. God shall bless us."

"In all things Christ must have the preeminence!" This is what I wanted in my married life. And this woman had let me know that she also wanted all things to be unto the praise of His glory! I accepted the letters in place of the seeing-each-other ceremony, which sped up the process. Our parents and families made arrangements in Kerala for our marriage. I informed my friends and colleagues in Bombay and, after the families made all the arrangements, I arrived in Kerala on a Saturday, went to see the girl on Monday, and got married on the following Thursday!

What happened to my prayer request list? I had placed that list on the altar. When you lay anything on the altar, God accepts it and often gives us back some privileges. In my case God gave me more than what I had mentioned in my list. I asked for a girl with a degree in science; this woman already had obtained her master's degree in science. I asked for a girl who was able to sing well; she not only sang but also directed a choir. And she had been involved in leading Bible studies for girls on campus even during her student days.

In addition, this wonderful woman who is my wife was

able to edit, which she had been doing for years, and which she has done for me with this book. God gave me more in her than I had desired in my own list of a wife's qualifications. Yes, God is interested in giving you more than you can think or imagine, and so we can truly trust Him and seek His will in all aspects of life.

CREATED FOR EACH OTHER

Many people have asked me if Elizabeth and I felt strange because we had not had an opportunity to be together before our marriage. The fact is that we did not feel like strangers. We began to talk as if we had known each other for many years. Of course, we both had known the same intimate Friend, Jesus Christ, for many years. We both wanted to copy some of His character traits in our lives. This God-factor made a difference.

Sadly, many people today leave the God-factor out. God is definitely interested in your well-being. He wants to show His greatness through your family. Whatever the psychological makeup of a couple, you can remember that God has designed every family with great potential to glorify Him.

It is true that many people take the factors of health, wealth, status, and other things into mind when considering marriage. Many also consider the God-factor, but only for their own material prosperity. When such people experience material loss, they question God and at times even blame Him. If we entrust God with anything, we can be assured that everything will be perfect. It may not be perfect according to our terms, but we must remember that we have a limited perspective. God makes everything perfect on His terms.

Because God is going to supply what you lack, you can relax in Him. Because you have a God-arranged marriage, you don't need to be worried about what the husband or wife is going to do to you or against you. In this context, a God-arranged marriage means an arrangement that involves the "Altar Test." The Altar Test is when both parties lay everything on the altar and give up their rights and expectations. In a way, a God-arranged marriage is like purifying gold in the furnace, where the altar burns away all the unwanted elements and leaves only the best.

Elizabeth and I wanted to seek God's kingdom first through our life together. It was a thrilling and encouraging experience to be with friends who sincerely prayed for us and wished us God's best. Some people, of course, misunderstand God's best because they only view it in terms of material benefits. We knew we were going to have an exciting future because we had several friends who had prayed for us. That made us think of all the things we could do in the future, with the knowledge of supportive prayers from sincere friends, a great family heritage, education, and all the abilities God had given us.

We were well received by our friends in the church and our social circle. We were given opportunities to exercise leadership, which helped build our confidence. We wanted to be an example of a deeply spiritual couple, and so we began to model everything we did with this in mind. On the whole, everything was going well. We lived such busy lives that we did not pay much attention to the minor things that did not go so well. However, those minor matters began to bother me.

I was of the impression that we both were prepared by God in a special way for each other, and that we were ready to set an example as a deeply spiritual family. After all, we were mature and needed to achieve so much for God through the many opportunities He had given us. We also sensed the need to get ourselves better equipped for God's work—although we felt our prayer life and our daily devotional life were strong, at least compared to normal standards. So why did minor matters begin to bother me so much?

For example, one of those minor matters concerned what we did at the breakfast table. During those early days, we enjoyed a quick breakfast of bread, butter, jam, boiled egg, and so forth. I was in the habit of covering the butter dish or placing the lid over the jam bottle when I had taken a little to put on my bread. My wife, however, was used to not closing them until breakfast was over. I didn't like to see the butter dish and the jam bottle left open. I did not want to tell her about it and force her to change her habit, but I did wish she would close them up the way I liked it! The best way to deal with this for me was to close them gently myself every time I found them left open. I hoped she would follow my good example in a few days. When this didn't happen, I figured she had not gotten the message. I began to close the containers more forcefully to produce a good clinking noise! This would let her know how I wanted them closed.

But even that failed to produce the results I wanted. My wife still left the jars and butter dish uncovered. Now what was I supposed to do? Was I going to have to live with such an experience all my life? It's sad now to realize that even after having had a nice breakfast, the unclosed lids haunted my thoughts. I began to think about the lids even while I traveled to my office. She did not close them! She did not even have the sense to follow what I wanted! Why can't she close them?

I began to get worked up and irritated—and ended up getting on the wrong bus. My frustration continued to bother me even after I reached work. It affected my think-ing process, and I began to ask questions like: "Why did God give me this kind of wife? What happened to the prayers of so many friends? What meaning do those Bible verses assuring me of great promises have now? Is this the kind of wife God wanted me to have?"

It's amazing what kinds of things can make us believe our foundations are being shaken. We need to recognize that God has many ways of speaking to us. I learned from C. S. Lewis's book, *The Problem of Pain*, that God sometimes uses pain as a kind of megaphone to get our attention when He speaks to us. In this situation, God spoke to me and taught me some great and valuable lessons. In the midst of my agitation, He answered my angry questions. But the answer was far different from what I had expected. He told me, "Until you change your attitude, your wife will con-tinue to keep the butter dish and jam bottle opened. Until you change your attitude, until you stop getting agitated, until you view your wife differently . . . she will not close them!"

Now I could see more clearly what was happening. I had been saying I wanted to accomplish God's purposes in my life. God was testing my desires to accomplish the purposes He has given me by giving me the right kind of wife—one who would help me to see my own weaknesses and faults. God wanted to develop my personality, and He provided the right kind of tool with that purpose in mind. He was using my wife as a precious tool in His hands to chip away the rough edges of my personality. My pastor could not do it. My mentor could not do it. My supervisor at work could not do it. The best tool God could use was my own wife. With this in mind, I should not get worked up when we go through hard times. Instead, I must say: "Thank you, Lord, for my wife!"

It wasn't long before my wife discovered the very same thing, especially when I behaved contrary to her expectations. She also began to thank God for me. (She probably had to thank God more often, because of my rough and selfish nature!) Before marriage we were two; after marriage we became one. We both benefited from being used as God's tools on each other. I can boldly ask God what He is going to do in my life when I see something in my wife I don't agree with. In the same way, my wife also asks God the same question when she comes across negatives in my life. We can therefore accept each other rather than blame each other. It is exciting to experience God's work on your personality in such a manner.

FINDING AN EXCITING LIFE TOGETHER

Each of us is God's workmanship, and He has to use many kinds of tools on us. God uses circumstances, people, events, and incidents to chip away our rough edges. But your husband or wife is an irreplaceable tool. It is best to understand this from the very beginning and look forward to an exciting life together.

As I am writing this, Elizabeth and I have enjoyed over twenty-one years of married life. She tells me I am much better than her first husband! No, she was never married before. I am that first husband. And I am thankful that she believes I am much better now—and she doesn't mind when I say the same about her. We are being changed, day by day. More and more we recognize that even the bitter and painful experiences are there not to break us but to make us.

God is bringing us many challenges, opportunities and problems, obstacles, and unforeseen struggles. Through these things we are able to experience the power that strengthens us and to see how all things work together for good. We should not bear everything in a spirit of defeat; rather, we should enjoy a fulfilled life in spite of many unfulfilled expectations.

To get worked up over covering a butter dish and jam bottle may seem insignificant. But it was a tool God used to shape our character and teach us. He has also used larger, more serious, seemingly insolvable problems. Like many others, we faced financial stress and humiliating experiences. We also experienced misunderstanding and strain in our relationships. We were inconvenienced because of immature decisions. We nearly gave up when our prayers were not answered according to our expectations.

For example, within a few days of the birth of our oldest boy, we found him seriously ill. During the first eighteen months of his life, we had to move him from hospital to hospital. My wife had no time to rest after the delivery. In fact, we had to struggle with seeing our child battling for breath. Repeated illnesses and the strain of barely managing put pressure on our entire family.

After the delivery of our second child, my wife was out of the hospital in a few days—but the child passed away within two months. Our youngest boy was born prematurely and was kept in an incubator. Again we went through strain and tension in managing with this child, who suffered from the same threatening illness as his older brother, a rare disease known as mucoviscidosis, for which there is no curative therapy available in any part of the world! Then God gave us a daughter who is free from any of these threatening diseases. Out of our four children, only the girl is living a normal life.

While taking care of both the boys at home, my wife suffered from an ovarian cyst and a disease of the uterus.

She had to undergo abdominal surgery while I struggled with caring for the boys. It was a strain for both of us, for me in caring for two ill children, and for my wife who constantly thought of me taking care of the boys at home and looking after her in the hospital. On top of that, God had given us a ministry that was very demanding and that involved a lot of travel on my part. Because of this, my wife had to fill the roles of both mother and father for almost a hundred and sixty days every year. Then, when her father passed away six years ago, we experienced the additional strain of bearing the financial burden of running the ministry her father had founded.

Life-threatening situations and discouraging experiences are all part of our family life mosaic—but none of these things has defeated us. We refused to let fear, disappointments, and sicknesses defeat us. The Bible says: "But despite all this, overwhelming victory is ours through Christ who loved us enough to die for us" (Romans 8:37).

You may be wondering how we have survived. We are being helped by an almighty, all-loving God in all these situations. Even now, as our children continue to have problems and medical specialists give us news that is not very encouraging, we know we are not alone. God is with us. He has worked the miracle of letting our oldest boy live to celebrate his nineteenth birthday—something the doctors told us probably would not happen. Our thirteen-year-old boy faces the same discouraging prognosis . . . but we believe in a God of impossibilities. And He has never let us down!

We never imagined we would go through these experiences. But God has delivered us in the midst of our troubles! God not only delivers us *in* the troubles, but He also delivers us *from* the troubles. I have already shared with you how God has delivered me from some of the difficulties I have faced.

Because we know we can rely on God and His deliverance, we can courageously face all discouraging situations. Sometimes there may not be any solution to the problem we face. We may not be able to do anything when the wind blows in different directions—but we can adjust the sails, and trust our Navigator to take full advantage of the direction it blows.

8

Pleasing God in All Things—Is It Possible?

THE BIRTH OF OUR FIRST CHILD

My wife and I wanted to please God in all things. Because of this, we knew it was important to work on our relationships with others, to keep those relationships within the lines of God's will. Though we felt confident in our direction and decisions, we often sought the opinion of others to be sure we were doing what God wanted of us. We found the counsel of others helpful, and it pleased us to hear people speak well of us and our ministry. As we became more popular among our peers and the community at large, we developed two specific patterns: We did our best to trust God in all things, and we sought to follow God's will in all circumstances.

We wanted to do our best for God. We did all we could to bring glory to God in our various involvements. The messages and testimonies we heard in conferences impacted me greatly. I wanted to do the maximum for God, just as these other leaders were doing. Furthermore, we wanted to be worthy of the prayer support we knew we were receiving from people in Kerala, other parts of India, and around the world.

We felt we were international in our contacts and outlook. At the same time, we were sure that our main contributions would be to the people of our own country, India. Thinking internationally and being Indian was a comfortable experience. Our vision was not limited, and we looked to the future with great expectations. Because our ambition and expectations were relative to the spiritual contributions we intended to make, we visualized everything in that dimension—even having children.

When we knew that we were going to have our first child, I looked in the Bible and found a name for him. I named him John as we read, "Your wife Elizabeth will bear you a son! And you are to name him John" (Luke 1:13). I had every expectation that our child would be a boy—and it was. The staff nurse asked me the name of the child to be entered in the hospital register soon after the delivery. I told her to write, "John George Samuel, baby of Elizabeth and George Samuel."

All the family, especially the grandparents, were happy to hear that it was a normal delivery and that it was a boy. This was the first grandchild in both families. Our friends also were happy, and a number of them came to the hospital and offered prayers of thanksgiving. Everything seemed normal with the child. The next morning, however, the doctor told us that he suspected the child was struggling and had some breathing problem. The problem persisted, and the child was given antibiotics. Not only did the breathing problem persist even after a course of injections, the child could not suck because of heavy nasal congestion. He could not swallow anything, even when he was spoon-fed.

Our baby was becoming dehydrated, and so tube-feeding was begun. Another course of antibiotic injections was given, and still the problem persisted. I had to rush to the hospital from a convention at which I was speaking. The doctors told us they suspected a fistula, a relatively rare congenital abnormality in which there is a passage between the foodpipe and the windpipe. They explained that the saliva flowed into our son's lungs, causing congestion and infection. The only way to correct it was by thoracic surgery. The staff suggested we take our baby to C.M.C. Hospital in Vellore, over 550 kilometers (about 350 miles) away.

Elizabeth and I were frantic. How could we take this sick child, ten days after his birth, all the way to Vellore? The grandparents, other relatives, several friends, and other visitors came to the ward. All were looking at me, waiting to hear my decision. What would be best for little John? Would C.M.C. Vellore be the answer? Would this sick child survive the trip to Vellore? Would he survive surgery?

I remembered the prayers we had prayed together prior to our son's birth. My wife and I had said that the child belonged to God and that although he would be our son, we would only be given the stewardship duty of raising him up for God. In our prayer, we had told the Lord that the child was on the altar, the same way Abraham had laid Isaac on the altar.

Perhaps the Lord is checking on me, I thought, *to see if I really meant that prayer.* Sometimes we give things to God in prayer, but we don't really mean it. We are praying from what we think we are supposed to say rather than from the heart. But when issues and situations like this come up, we have to know how serious we were in our commitment.

Finally, I decided it was not practical to take John immediately to Vellore. We requested the hospital authorities to allow us to keep him there. Soon, John began to suffer from severe chest infection. And he went through the dreadful experience of cyanosis, in which he turned blue because of breathlessness. Oxygen was available only in the operating room, so the nurses had to regularly race there carrying our breathless child! We did not know whether the child would breathe again until he was handed back to us.

This happened over and over; sometimes the waiting was long because of severe congestion caused by the infection. The doctors who attended the situation had to do mouth-to-mouth resuscitation and cardiac massage. On a number of occasions, it took a long time to revive John. The doctors warned us that oxygen deprivation could cause severe brain damage.

At least two people were watching around the clock for changes in our baby's appearance. If he was left unnoticed and became cyanosed, the result would be fatal. Even after bringing him back through resuscitation, there was always the possibility of a relapse. My wife was constantly with him, watching every change so she could immediately rush him to the operating room if needed. Because of pharyngeal secretions, he used to get choked and cyanosed even while he cried.

Often we had to let him sleep in a slanted position because we feared he would choke from the secretions. One evening, the senior doctors were about to leave for a function outside the hospital, which left one junior doctor available, when John again became cyanotic. He was rushed to the operating room. He needed mouth-to-mouth resuscitation, but this junior doctor and the nurses were hesitant to do it on such a tiny child. We knew John was moments from death. But one of the sisters ran and got the senior doctor just before he left the building, and our child was again revived. Thus he "died" several times.

We stayed in the hospital for five and a half months, facing problems day and night. We praise God for the many people who supported us by their presence, prayer, and labor of love. We were not discouraged. We hoped that when John put on some weight, he might tolerate an operation, and so we waited before taking him to Vellore. But those five and a half months in the hospital were an opportunity to trust God in a special way. We also felt we were undergoing some kind of special theological training in the hospital during these experiences.

SPIRITUAL TRAINING IN THE HOSPITAL WARD

My wife and I wanted to get the best training we could for the exciting future before us. What we didn't realize was that that was exactly what God was giving us through our experiences with our first child! We received special training that you could never find in any theological institution. So we praise God for those experiences.

When we finally decided to take John to Vellore, we thought the problem would be solved. Once there, the thoracic surgeon told us he could not do the operation unless the fistula between the trachea and esophagus was confirmed by the radiologist. The radiologist looked for such a passage or fistula through special diagnostic procedures, but he could not see even a sign of such a passage. So they advised us to spoon-feed him and give him a semisolid diet at home.

It was a great relief to be able to take John home. But within a few days, he began to get dehydrated, and so he once again needed to be tube fed and given intravenous fluids. We thought we could manage by taking him to a hospital as an outpatient once in a while. We also kept our eyes open for a child specialist in our area. When someone told us of any new child specialist, we were eager to go and consult him. We thought a newly appointed and highly qualified child specialist in a nearby hospital might help us. He expressed his willingness to do so, but John was getting weaker. Another generous child specialist did all he could to help us, and so we once again took John to a hospital far away. Our friends in that town and the prayers of our friends encouraged us a lot.

Again the doctors could reach no definite diagnosis. But the medical personnel helped to control the infection and maintain John through special care. It was convenient to move him back to a nearby hospital where the child specialist was available. Moving back and forth from hospital to hospital, returning to the same hospital without knowing what could be done, and not being certain of what would happen next pervaded our minds, as well as the minds of our friends and relatives.

In a situation like this, when doctors fail to find a solution, it's amazing how many people offer opinions. This brought us new difficulties. When people are confused and see no light at the end of the tunnel, some of their opinions hurt. We saw concern, sympathy, pride, superiority complexes, inferiority complexes, spiritualizing of issues, supernatural intervention, rebuke, exhortation, and all manner of things, both useful and unwanted, coming at us.

For example, one surgeon claimed he found the tracheoesophageal fistula during bronchoscopy and wanted to operate on the child then and there! He began to tell our relatives and visitors that we were taking our son to the grave if we did not hand him over into his hands for the operation. People with common sense naturally question such a claim. How could this doctor have found something specialists could not find using specialized equipment? However, we were in great need. Here was someone offering his help. Moreover, he was trying to persuade people to influence us to heed his advice. Here again opinions differed; some were in favor, others were not. So strain and stress came at us from many directions.

We longed for the day we could take John home. The hospital staff were generous and helpful in letting us keep John there, but it was a difficult situation at best. In those days, warm water for John, as well as hot water for baths, had to be carried to the hospital from home. We all eagerly waited for the day when John could be taken home and cared for there. After months of prayer and waiting, our baby boy was discharged, not because he was cured, but because my wife had learned how to tube feed! We had already learned how to give him antibiotics orally, and we could aspirate secretions using an electrical device. Now we could feed him by tube to avoid dehydration and associated problems.

Caring for our baby at home meant watching him day and night, feeding him properly, and taking care to see that he would not get severe infections leading to cyanosis. If the feeding tube went into the windpipe instead of the stomach, he would be in serious trouble. As we did not have anyone who was experienced in such things nearby, we developed more trust and confidence in the One who is in control of all things. We knew we were not alone!

In reading about our experiences, you may be wondering what happened to the prayers of many people for this child. Yes, many people sincerely and faithfully prayed and are still praying. The fact that we were all kept safe and in good shape, mentally and spiritually, is an answer to their prayers. We could have become consumed by bitterness over how our family life started, and frustration over wondering what had happened to our great plans. But through everything, my wife and I know that the God who gave us all of our good desires was aware of the entire situation. In fact, we believe God allowed all of this to happen. We know that what happens to us is not so important; what happens through us is more important! What God does in us through all of our tension-mounting experiences is of greater value than the distressing events and problems.

Resources to Counteract Hardships

Imagine going into the hospital to deliver your first child and not returning home with the child until eleven months later! As you can imagine, this experience was very difficult for my wife. But she *did* return home with our son, and that fact alone is a miracle. Of course, life was far from easy. We could feed John only by risky tube-feeding. We gave him semisolids, jelly, and some fruit juice little by little, spoon by spoon, taking great care to prevent aspiration which would result in chest infection. John's mealtimes lasted several hours because someone had to follow him with food to feed him a little at a time. But our main concern was to keep him at home without hospitalization. Finally, after he was eighteen months old, we could discontinue using the tube. Even then he was only slowly putting on weight.

My wife was eager to study in a Bible school or theological seminary. She never gave up that hope, in spite of the child's prolonged sickness. In fact, arrangements were made for her to study Bible and theology courses in California. We hoped that when John could eat normal food, he also could be with her in California. But he was not getting well enough to travel. We went ahead with the travel and medical treatment arrangements. We paid the airfare several months in advance, working it out that my wife and child could travel with some friends who would be taking that same plane. But the time for the trip grew near, and John's health still was not good enough.

One day my wife was thinking of her proposed Bible

school studies. During a casual conversation, a servant of God talked about people whom God used without such formal Bible school training, including himself. That day my wife decided to give up her ambition of joining any Bible school or seminary. She thanked the Lord for the two years of "intensive training" she already had received in the hospital and in caring for John at home. She already had served the basic training and was satisfied that God used that as a foundation for additional advanced training.

John was over two years old when he and my wife joined me in California. Our first goal was to get our son thoroughly examined. He was still sick, but we thought we could manage. The specialists who examined John could not find any of those suspected passages between the trachea and esophagus. In fact, they could not diagnose his problems. So they asked us about the medical history and finally said he might outgrow the problems.

In many respects, life was convenient and comfortable in California. But we were restricted because of John's illness. He was being cared for by several people at home, and we soon became aware that his health was deteriorating more quickly than it had when two of us looked after him. That meant our son was still sick and was suffering from some major problems. But, try as they might, even the great specialists could not find the cause.

In light of all we faced, one might get the impression that we were a very unlucky couple. This is a difficult thing for many Christians, especially since so many think that only those who live outside God's will run into these kinds of difficulties. But this is not so. The Scriptures tell us very clearly that hard times will come to Christians and non-Christians alike (see Matthew 5:45).

My wife and I have been very aware of this, and I can

honestly say that never in our life together, especially during those difficult years, did we curse God or doubt His sovereignty. We surely took time to examine our lives, and we benefited much from such self-examinations. Our hands and pockets were becoming empty, but our hearts were always full! If nothing else, we have learned that what you do with what happens matters a lot.

Are you faced with trials and difficulties? Don't be upset. Instead, feed on the spiritual food that is so freely available in God's Word and find nourishment to strengthen you and help you while you undergo all kinds of trouble. By the time God delivered His people from Pharaoh, they were already strong because they had developed their muscles through hard work. Those hardships enabled them to be strong. Generally, hardships are not physical. They most often are psychological, emotional, relational, or financial. Or they may be a combination of some or all of these things. In certain cases, they may raise unanswerable questions. That's understandable. Don't worry about these questions, for you will know the answers in the right time. Just keep moving forward in God's will, and trust Him for the final outcome.

As you go through trials, you probably will find yourself re-evaluating your goals and setting new priorities. This is a good step. After all, we have only one life to live, and we need to live it for God. I remember an old story of a little child who was given a penny by her mother to buy candy. She took a long time to select the candy of her choice. When the mother told her to hurry up, she said: "Mummy, I only have one penny." She wanted to spend it wisely. We do not have much time to waste worrying about distressing experiences. Because God is with us, we can know we are not going to be defeated. Jesus said: "Here on earth you will have many trials and sorrows; but cheer up, for I have overcome the world" (John 16:33). No matter what happens to you—whether death in the family, threatening illness, or additional tribulations—with God, you will not be defeated! I can say this with confidence because I know it to be true—as you will see.

9

No Ownership— Only Stewardship

As I mentioned before, our second child, Sherry, died. When he was born, we had no idea there would be any problems. Elizabeth gave birth to Sherry a few minutes after being taken to the labor room of the hospital. Johny, our older child, was so happy to hear about the birth of his younger brother. He loved him very much. As for my wife and me, we were greatly relieved when mother and child were discharged from the hospital within the normal time period. Now my wife was taking care of our two children in Kerala while I had to be in California for a few more months.

During this time, within a two week period, Sherry suddenly developed respiratory problems. He could suck and take in fluid, but only at a low rate. Then he, like his older brother, suffered a cyanotic attack because of choking. Soon he experienced a respiratory infection that required hospitalization.

The problems multiplied. Johny needed attention at home, and Sherry needed Elizabeth in the hospital. Johny turned three while Sherry was in the hospital with respiratory infection. Finally, Sherry improved, and when it was possible to manage him at home, he was discharged from the hospital. Johny was thrilled to see his brother back home.

It was only a few days later that Sherry developed further breathing difficulties. Suddenly he became breathless and blue and was rushed to the hospital. The doctors examined him—and pronounced him dead of severe respiratory infection. I was away in California. Elizabeth's parents had taken the train for an important meeting in Madras that day. The stationmaster of Salem railway station—where their train arrived around midnight—was contacted. We were grateful to the railway staff, who took the pain to locate Elizabeth's parents on the train, wake them, and arrange for their return so they could be home the following morning. Many difficult things had to be done, but God arranged for all the people to be where they needed to be at the right time. Some dear people in the neighborhood accompanied Elizabeth and our sick child to the hospital. After Sherry's death, these dear friends took care of many of the funeral arrangements.

I often think of the orange tree in the yard where I lived in California. At various times, I could see tiny oranges that were unripe, ripe, and very ripe. I used to pluck one or two from among the tiny and unripe ones, just to hold them in my hands. I had the freedom to pluck these oranges, just as God is free to exercise His will in His universe. God is infinite in His wisdom, and we are not able to fathom the meaning of all that He allows into our lives—including sickness and death. If I believe God is able to make *all* things work together for good, I must accept that that includes afflictions and death. And we are, in part, made and remade through these experiences.

The apostle Paul said: "For I am convinced that nothing can ever separate us from his love. Death can't, and life can't" (Romans 8:38). Our children are God's gift to us, but the owner is still God. We are only stewards to raise them up for God. We gave up all our rights to our children when we placed them on the altar. He is in control of their lives. Every aspect of them. He is there, with our children, watching over them, caring for them, working His will in their lives. We can do more for them by surrendering them to an almighty God than we can do in our own strength.

A Third Birth—And Good News

Eventually, Elizabeth, Johny and I settled in Kerala to build a ministry in our land. Shortly thereafter, our daughter, Annie, was born. When we noticed a little extra pharyngeal secretion in a couple of days of her birth, we all suspected that she was in the same boat as her brothers. Happily, it was something else, a problem often seen in any normal child. Soon we received the glad news that Annie was a healthy, normal child. How grateful we all were!

It's true that we thanked God for his mercy and grace in granting us a healthy child. But we kept in mind this fact: a healthy, normal child also belongs to God. Here again, we are only stewards to take care of her, and so we placed her on the altar, too. Yes, we were glad our daughter was healthy. But we could be truly happy only if our child's health, abilities, and life were in God's hands. God seeks to use everybody, both healthy and unhealthy, for the work of His kingdom.

The way in which you use your health, wealth, and education matters a lot. If your life is of no use in light of God's kingdom, if you are living just for yourself, you are living without real purpose. A worthwhile question to ask ourselves is, "Am I giving my best for the kingdom of God?" Without God at the center of all we are and do, we can never be truly happy.

When our oldest son was almost seven years old, we had our fourth and final child. At this time, Johny was going to school under special care because of his poor health and Annie was growing up as a normal, healthy child. When our last boy, Ronnie, was born, he was five weeks premature. His birth weight was so low that the hospital staff had to give him special care. Elizabeth was discharged from the hospital within the normal time, but our tiny little boy was kept in an incubator for a month. There were times we all wondered whether he could survive.

We asked the doctors if Ronnie was experiencing any respiratory problems. Sadly, the doctor's answer was affirmative: Ronnie suffered from the same illness as his two brothers. We prayed, asking God not to give us another eleven months in the hospitals with him. We tried to provide sterile conditions at home to prevent further hospitalization after we brought him home. We tried to manage Ronnie at home since his sickness was not so intense as his brothers'. He was (and still is) very slow in putting on weight. Occasionally we had to call the specialist to our home to check on his condition and administer antibiotics.

When Ronnie was nearing his second birthday, he fell very ill. I was in Singapore attending a meeting when I received a phone call informing me of the seriousness of his attack. He had already been hospitalized and was sinking fast. I rushed back and found him weak and sick. After several days of treatment for respiratory infection and subsequent dehydration, he was brought home. Again we worked to maintain a sterile condition at home to prevent further infection and relapse. Slowly Ronnie's health improved.

A few weeks later, I had to leave for Bhubaneswar for a series of meetings. At these meetings, I spoke emphatically about "all things work together for good." One day I visited some friends in town. When I returned, I walked straight into the evening meeting. As I took my seat they were in the middle of an ardent prayer in the local language. I could not follow the prayer since that local language is so different from mine. But I was surprised to hear my name mentioned.

I could not ask anyone sitting nearby why my name had been mentioned because they were all praying intently. As I listened, I realized that the speaker was also uttering the word for child in his language. I thought the organizers might have received some telephone message during my absence regarding Ronnie. In my mind, I began making plans to return home to be with my wife and children. As soon as that dear man finished the prayer, I asked one of the leaders why my name was mentioned in the prayer. His reply was that the person was quoting part of the message I had given the previous night, that is, "all things work together for good," when they prayed for the sick child of one of the organizers there!

Here I was, the preacher, caught in turmoil while the people who had heard me speak were encouraged and strengthened. I recalled the words of the apostle Paul: "I don't mean to say I am perfect. I haven't learned all I should even yet, but I keep working towards that day when I will finally be all that Christ saved me for and wants me to be" (Philippians 3:12).

I am glad God is not yet finished with me, that He is still working on me. And I know He will complete the picture one day. "I am sure that God who began the good work within you will keep right on helping you grow in his grace until his task within you is finally finished on that day when

Jesus Christ returns" (Philippians 1:6).

I am humbled and encouraged that God can speak through me, despite my weaknesses. I am in His hands. He is always present, caring for me and watching out for me. No matter what happens, I am not alone. "Shall I look to the mountain gods for help? No! My help is from Jehovah who made the mountains! And the heavens too! He will never let me stumble, slip or fall. For he is always watching, never sleeping. Jehovah himself is caring for you! He is your defender. He protects you day and night. He keeps you from all evil and preserves your life. He keeps his eye upon you as you come and go and always guards you" (Psalm 121:1–8).

THE STRAIN BEGINS TO TELL

Elizabeth and I don't believe in fate, we believe in God's plan. Elizabeth has always been very involved in our work. She taught degree-level classes in college, she helped students spiritually in their character development, she devoted time for music and ministry among women and youth in the church. Now she was caring for her sick children! Day and night, she engaged in a battle for life and breath for her own children. She had to forgo meals, her bath, and other essentials of daily life. She had to be ready to rush to the hospital at any time. All without any encouragement from the doctors or specialists that things would eventually change or get better. I could go to a meeting and receive sympathy and the comforting fellowship of several dear friends, but she was shut up in the hospital or the sick room, often watching the boys gasping for breath.

Yet, in the midst of it all, Elizabeth was always sure of her commitment to God. She often said: "I have given myself to God, it is God's responsibility to take care of the rest." Her talents in singing, Bible teaching, and organizing programs for women and youth were all included when she committed herself to God. He could use those talents in more blessed ways than we could ever imagine. Elizabeth recognized that God not only ordains pastors and bishops, but He also ordains people to serve Him in all situations and circumstances. Along with this ordination comes the strength and the power and the courage to face whatever comes.

Elizabeth did not accept God's will in her life with a long, disappointed face. Rather, she always had an assurance that flowed as a result of the gentle touch of God's loving hand. Although one of her children had died, she never lost her hope. She believed that God's power could step in at any time. Her hope was not in what the world could provide, but in an almighty God.

She was so firm in her faith that she was always involved in the business of the kingdom of God. She was with me in my work; I could go around the world several times a year only with her strong backing and support. All who know our situation are aware of the fact that she was the one who actually underwent the major parts of suffering and afflictions, but she never complained. She is the most fulfilled person I know, living a fulfilled life despite what many in the world might think were unfulfilled rights and privileges. She lacks nothing, because she has given herself to a God who gives her all she needs.

THE CHILDREN GROW IN FAITH

You may be wondering about our children. Many have been curious as to how they have reacted to their lot in life, or how they respond when they see children of their ages play and travel.

In the same way that God has cared for Elizabeth and me, He also has cared for our children. Nothing we can do will compensate for or equal what our children see in normal children. But God compensates His little ones fully! Our children have a firm faith in God—not a faith that was imposed on them but one that they developed themselves. They believe God is able to heal them and provide for them. They are eager to attend school and score high marks like the other children.

They are, of course, limited in many ways because of their illness. But they are keenly aware of victory. Swallowing food without throwing up makes them often say, "Praise the Lord." Often they thank and praise God in advance for not letting the food come back up. This was not a kind of make-believe that they indulged in. Rather, they began early to subject their beliefs to the test of experience. It is through this trusting process that they are growing up. Severe pain, suffocation, and sleeplessness are difficult to bear. Our boys have learned to pray with tears of aches and pain.

In addition, our children pray for others in need. Once a young man who came to attend a Bible seminar in our center was bedridden because of some sickness. Johny went and prayed for him, and this young man got up from the bed and walked. Another time my mother was bedridden with severe arthritis. She could not move her arms or feet. Johny and Ronnie laid their hands on her and prayed. A few minutes later, my mother could bend her arm to chase a mosquito away from her nose! This encouraged her to try to get up, which she did, saying, "My little children prayed for me and God healed me."

When Johny was about four years old, I came home from a conference with an eye infection. Seeing my red eye, Johny asked me to pray to Jesus who healed a blind man.

Someone had narrated a Bible story to him and, seeing my minor eye problem, he remembered it. Johny joined me when I prayed in the evening for my eye trouble. A little later Johny climbed onto the bed I used in another room. I advised him not to come near me for fear he would catch the eye infection from me. He immediately asked why I was worried when we had prayed to Jesus for healing! I had to confess my lack of faith to my son and pray again with him, believing like a child. The result of that prayer was that the infection was gone when I got up the next morning.

Of course, we do not attribute any superhuman power to our children. They are simply small, often sick, children. But they know and trust a God who is able to heal and encourage—a God who can even raise the dead! Remember what Jesus said? "I tell you as seriously as I know how that anyone who refuses to come to God like a little child will never be allowed into his kingdom" (Mark 10:15).

This is indeed a spiritual exercise for the entire family. Do not discount or ignore what God is doing in and through your children. He can use even powerless sick children to shape our lives.

10

God's Power
Never Ceases

Most of us, including the doctors, were under the impression that the boys would outgrow their illness. The only thing we really had to do was to administer medication every time Johny and Ronnie had an infection or other major medical difficulty.

When Johny turned eleven years old, we noticed that when he had a chest infection, he often became severely dehydrated from diarrhea and vomiting. He was growing weak and losing weight.

One Sunday afternoon in April of 1982, Johny fell very ill. After vomiting for several hours, he fell unconscious. We tried the usual methods of shaking him and giving gun steam inhalations to clear the breathing passages. But this time his condition continued in spite of all our efforts. We rushed him to the hospital where he was admitted to the intensive care unit. Chest X-rays revealed a severe lung infection. They discovered that practically 80 percent of his lung had turned fibroid because of the repeated respiratory infections during all those years.

The X-ray results were so discouraging that the doctors feared tuberculosis. They put Johny, who was still unconscious, on strong antibiotics. Although he was kept under constant vigil by the faithful nurses, the comatose condition continued and we were warned that Johny might never open his eyes again. He was sinking fast. Both Elizabeth and I accepted it as God's will. We thought it was better that God would call him home rather than let him suffer here with tuberculosis and meningitis.

We immediately made arrangements to check the other children for tuberculosis. Although Ronnie was not as sick as Johny, he looked like a TB patient, especially when he didn't cover his chest. The following morning we returned home early from the intensive care unit. During our family prayer, we happened to read a passage from James's letter, "For the Lord will make him well" (James 5:15). To us this Bible verse was like holding out a piece of straw to help save a drowning person. However, we decided to hold onto it tightly and prayed for God's will to happen.

Always before, someone in our family had stayed with Johny, whether he was in the hospital ward or at home. This time, because of the rules of the intensive care unit, none of us were there. I was concerned that he might regain consciousness, look for his mom or any one of us, and then scream and get upset when he couldn't find us there. Forty-eight hours after he was admitted to the intensive care unit and twenty-four hours after we had received the assurance from God's Word, I went to the hospital to see how he was doing.

I entered his room just as he slowly opened his eyes and called me. "Daddy," he said, then asked for his mother. I was overcome with joy and gratitude. God had not only brought Johny back to us, He had arranged for me to be there at the right time when he opened his eyes and came out of the coma.

Now that Johny was conscious, the doctors tested his spinal fluid to check for meningitis. All the tests proved negative. When Johny was maintained by intravenous fluid along with antibiotics, his general condition improved. But he was vomiting whenever the administration of electrolytes ceased. From a blood test, we discovered that infection was depleting his sodium level. Further testing by a specialist revealed that Johny's diarrhea was due to pancreatic insufficiency. Both conditions began to clear up with treatment.

Later the dear child specialist who treated Johny came to talk with us. He had spent hours going through textbooks and literature that described a very rare problem known as mucoviscidosis, or cystic fibrosis. In this condition, infants secret a fluid so thick that they find it difficult to bring it out. As a result, they often die of choking. Some of these thick secretions remain in the respiratory tract and get infected, causing repeated respiratory infection.

In India, cystic fibrosis is very rare. Children who are born with this problem usually die in early infancy either by choking or by infection. The child specialist explained the details to us, stating that there was no known cure for the condition. All we could do was treat the symptoms as they occurred.

Using my contacts worldwide, especially those in the medical profession, I started to collect research papers about this sickness. But all the specialists I contacted could only sympathize with me. They all agreed: there was no cure.

One specialist explained it to me this way: "Assume that something is wrong with a building. If it is just some of the walls, they can be replaced. But think of the difficulty if every brick used for the building will have to be replaced! It is easier to demolish the building and build a new one."

Demolish the building! I knew we could not do that

with my dear children. So I continued to collect any literature I could find about cystic fibrosis. I found that it is not
a rare sickness among the Caucasian populations. In fact,
there are many cystic fibrosis centers in the Western countries. But even in these centers there is no known cure, only
supportive therapy and medical advice on how to manage
such patients at home. There are also humanitarian organizations, such as the Cystic Fibrosis Foundation, which
support research and development. Their literature and
information on therapy were useful and informative—but
no one talked about a cure. More explanations were given
on how deterioration takes place with time, and so there is
not much hope.

While scanning through these research papers, my attention was drawn to a passage in the Bible: "For I can do
everything God asks me to with the help of Christ who
gives me the strength and power" (Philippians 4:13). I
thought about what it was saying. Jesus Christ never ceases
to make me able! So I can not only do everything God asks
me to do, but I also can bear all things God asks me to bear.
When the specialists say there is no hope for children with
cystic fibrosis and that the children die soon, I can bear all
such things because of the One who never ceases to make
me able.

Again, faith in crisis is subjecting our beliefs to the test
of experience. We have to experiment and prove whether
the One who never ceases to make us able steps in. We also
have to prove for our own personal conviction whether we
are able to bear affliction.

God Is Always in Control

During a trip for a meeting abroad, I arranged to go
through Los Angeles where some specialists agreed to look

at the boys' X-rays and medical reports. In fact, Johny's chest X-rays could be compared with the old pictures taken while he was in California several years ago. The specialists in Los Angeles were shocked to hear that the diagnosis was cystic fibrosis. In those days they did not suspect this for a patient from India and therefore had not tested for it.

I visited some cystic fibrosis centers in the United States and the United Kingdom during that trip. While I was getting ready to visit a center in London, word reached me from home saying, "Johny is critically ill." I was several thousand miles away, and I could not get through on the phone to find out his condition.

I flew toward London with mixed feelings. I very much wanted to be present if something bad already had happened. I had a six-hour layover in London, where I wanted to consult with one of the eminent specialists in a children's hospital. This specialist suggested we give Johny inhalation therapy. To do this, we needed to buy an electronic nebulizer. As I was placing the order, the salesman told me that a unit was available right there! So I bought it and the medications needed for the therapy, and went back to the airport to resume my flight.

When I arrived home, I found that Johny had experienced severe problems. He was recovering, but still terribly weak. We began using the equipment and medications I had brought home. As a result, we were able to prevent further hospitalization of both the children!

None of us had known what sickness we had been dealing with for so many years—twelve years for Johny and five years for Ronnie. I'm sure that, out of ignorance, we did several things we should not have done. But now we could seek help from specialists at cystic fibrosis centers abroad. Elizabeth did everything the specialists told her to do, and eventually could handle both the boys at the same time.

Because I had to travel a lot, I used to pack my suitcase and wait to get an OK from Johny as to whether or not I could go. If he felt things were bad enough, I would not go. He very much wanted me to be home during his funeral. I remember him looking at me with his very weak eyes and telling me, "Daddy, I am slightly better, so you may go." You can imagine how much strain this put on me as I traveled. The stress and strain wore Elizabeth and me down—but we did not lose heart. We often remembered this Bible passage:

> Everyone can see that the glorious power within must be from God and is not our own. We are pressed on every side by troubles, but not crushed and broken. We are perplexed because we don't know why things happen as they do, but we don't give up. We are hunted down, but God never abandons us. We get knocked down, but we get up again and keep going (2 Corinthians 4:7–9).

No matter what happened, we knew we were not going to be defeated. We were not facing our problems alone—we had the help of our all-powerful God.

TIMELY HELP

We praise God for those who willingly helped us day and night. We are thankful for the people who prayed for us. Several used to visit us in the hospital and at home to pray for us. Many wrote, assuring us of their continued prayers. In fact, people around the world are praying for us even now.

Leaders from Asia, Africa, and Latin America used to come to Singapore for the Haggai Institute Seminars. Because I am so close to the Haggai Institute's training ministry, having been associated with it since 1974, thousands of those committed men and women of God pray for us. Dr. John Haggai himself encouraged us as he and his wife, Christine, went through similar experiences for twenty-four years with their only son, Johnny. When men of God such as Dr. John Haggai speak to us from their experience, we get strengthened. We especially found encouragement and strength through Dr. Haggai's best-selling *How to Win Over Worry.*

Dr. DeLores Johnson, former professor of nuclear medicine at University of California School of Medicine and chief of nuclear medicine of Harbor General Hospital, Torrance, took special interest in arranging the medical tests for Johny. She also kept track of the best advice and medicine from the Cystic Fibrosis Center in Los Angeles.

Churches around the world, including at least a few in all continents, prayed. One church that has been praying for us for over eighteen years is Rolling Hills Covenant Church in Los Angeles, which I started attending while I headed a nuclear medicine department in a hospital in that area. Many friends from World Vision, Prison Fellowship, Living Bibles International, World Health Organization, United Nations—all had a soft corner for us in their hearts. In addition, those who heard my messages on various occasions backed us with prayer.

These people, and innumerable others, are angels God sent to minister to us. Not one of them can be forgotten. For when we remember all whom God has sent to pray for and help us, Elizabeth and I remember clearly that we did not do everything by ourselves or by our will power. We have always depended on the intercessory prayers of others. It is an incredible privilege to be backed by such a gathering of people around the world.

LEARNING TO TRUST GOD

One day while Elizabeth was caring for both of the boys, she complained of some abdominal pain. She went to a gynecologist who examined her, then told us Elizabeth had an enlarged ovarian cyst. The gynecologist told us to have the cyst removed by surgery as soon as possible, otherwise it might burst! After further examination the doctor suggested removing both the ovaries and the fibroid uterus completely—major surgery. We were stunned. How could Elizabeth go the hospital when she was the person who cared for the children?

We arranged for a private nurse to take care of Elizabeth while she was in the hospital, and I decided to look after the children. I prayed especially that God would not allow both children to be sick at the same time. Elizabeth can easily look after both simultaneously, but I can only handle one at a time.

Contrary to my expectation, things were different. Although everything went well in the hospital with the surgery, at home both boys became very sick at the same time. We had some people to help, but I had to stay awake at night and take care of them. During this time, God gave me something special from His Word: "Here he comes, leaping upon the mountains and bounding over the hills" (Song of Solomon 2:8) and "The Lord God is my Strength, and he will give me the speed of a deer and bring me safely over the mountains" (Habakkuk 3:19).

My problems may have been as big as the mountains, and my difficulties may have been as high as the hills, but the Lord could victoriously surmount all problems and difficulties. Not only did the Lord win, but He also made my feet like the feet of a deer to leap upon and skip upon these problems. How could God have shown me His sufficiency if only one of the children had been sick? He had to allow both to be sick for me to experience the greatness of His power.

Jesus invites us to experience victory *in* the troubles and *through* the troubles. We read in the gospel narratives:

> Jesus told his disciples to get into their boat and cross to the other side of the lake while he stayed to get the people started home. Then afterwards he went up into the hills to pray.
>
> Night fell, and out on the lake the disciples were in trouble. For the wind had risen and they were fighting heavy seas. About four o'clock in the morning Jesus came to them, walking on the water! They screamed in terror, for they thought he was a ghost. But Jesus immediately spoke to them, reassuring them. "Don't be afraid!" he said. Then Peter called to him: "Sir, if it is really you, tell me to come over to you walking on the water." "All right," the Lord said, "Come along!" So Peter went over the side of the boat and walked on the water towards Jesus (Matthew 14:22–29).

The disciples who were in trouble because of the rough sea saw Jesus overcoming all the storms and waves as He came toward them. He even allowed Peter to overcome all those big and dangerous high waves as well and walk toward Him. God wants us to win the victory on His terms. Later on, like Peter, we should not get terrified by all the afflictions and difficulties. Sometimes the victory will be in the troubles. We will benefit immensely as we go through situations that are humanly unbearable. In certain cases there will be victory from the troubles. We are not designed to get defeated by depression and fear. We are designed to win with God's strength and continuous empowerment.

Elizabeth was discharged from the hospital after successful surgery, and the boys were much better when she returned home. I wondered at that time at how much Elizabeth must have suffered all those years. But she says she was strengthened and empowered to carry a greater load. God is our strength. He surely makes our feet like those of the deer to leap over all the difficulties.

THE GOD WHO PROVIDES

The specialists who examined the medical reports of the children did not give us much hope. Johny's condition was very bad; they never expected him to live beyond nineteen. Ronnie's story would not be very different. But after coming out of the intensive care unit one time, Johny wrote on a display board: "What is impossible with man is possible with God."

If you came to our home, you would not see it as a distressing place or a house of disappointments. But you will see all of us rejoicing in God even while the children are sick with pain and discomfort. What Johny wrote with his very weak hands on the display board about the God of impossibilities can be seen hung on the front wall.

It is painful to think of your own children being taken away from this world, especially at an early age. The specialists have told us that the boys' internal organs are deteriorating instead of developing and growing. Due to malabsorption and sickness the nineteen-year-old boy weighs around twenty-nine kilograms (sixty-four pounds) and the thirteen-year-old boy about twenty kilograms (forty-four pounds) as I am writing this. Even if they put on a little weight, a minor infection could bring their weight back down.

Still, we are happy that their condition is improving day by day. They are not bedridden all the time. The younger boy attends school more or less regularly, although he doesn't have the stamina to study all the lessons. The older boy is allowed to attend school when he can, even if only for a few hours. The boys enjoy listening to music and seeing healthy children performing well in studies, sports, spiritual exercise, etc. We give them love and look after them as if they are going to live for many more years.

We were eagerly looking forward to Johny's nineteenth birthday. I prepared a birthday card for him four months in advance and wrote on it, "Today, January 21, 1989, Johny completed 19 years." It was something special for us to see him opening the cover and reading the card.

Sometimes, of course, discouraging questions arise. One day, leaning back in my chair, I began to wonder who would care for the boys after Elizabeth and I were gone. Unaware, tears started to trickle from my eyes. Then I felt as if God was talking to me: *"I, your God, am the One who provides even now; so after you are gone I will continue to provide for the children."* I had thought I was providing for the boys, and that I would have to provide for them as long as they lived. Now I know God is the Provider, now and always. Jesus had already told us,

> So my counsel is: Don't worry about *things*—food, drink, and clothes. For you already have life and a body—and they are far more important than what to eat and wear. Look at the birds! They don't worry about what to eat—they don't need to sow or reap or store up food—for your heavenly Father

feeds them. And you are far more valuable to him than they are. Will all your worries add a single moment to your life? (Matthew 6:25–27).

Johny copied a quotation and kept it on his desk: "It's bad if a man worries and loses his hair . . . it's worse still if he loses his head."

Johny's lung condition used to be very bad. Now the respiratory infection is controlled by supportive therapy. Nowadays he is generally free from stomach pain, diarrhea, and continuous vomiting. The boys regularly pray in faith. When some prayer requests are made known to the boys, they also pray for others very eagerly. Johny prays with much empathy because he has gone through severe afflictions himself. He reminds me that we are to pray in the name of Jesus, who also suffered: "For since he himself has now been through suffering and temptation, he knows what it is like when we suffer and are tempted, and he is wonderfully able to help us" (Hebrews 2:18).

When Johny reached his nineteenth birthday, in spite of the verdict of the specialists, we were reminded of the need to take steps of faith, despite what has happened in the past to disappoint us. We must not bury ourselves in our disappointments, shielding ourselves from ever taking a risk again. Instead, we must recognize that we can go on to accomplish God's will in our lives, with or without healing. Nowhere does it say that only normal, healthy people can accomplish higher things in life. What God does *through* you is surely more important than what happens *to* you.

You can have courage in time of discouragement. Your limitations, frustrations, and unfulfilled desires are not going to defeat you. Instead, they can become opportunities for new and thrilling discoveries.

11

Focus On Purpose

Pain Is Not Pain When We See the Purpose

I have learned from C. S. Lewis that pain is not pain when we see the purpose in it. We also know that pain without purpose is paralyzing.

In India we have many educated, unemployed youths, in spite of the fact that a number of them have gone to work in Middle Eastern countries. Just assume that one of those youths came to me one day when I was looking for someone to run an errand quite far away. Assume that no vehicles were allowed on the road that day due to some twenty-four-hour law. Now, suppose I wanted this young man to walk all the way, for six or seven hours at night, while heavy rains were pouring down, to collect an envelope containing some important documents. He would have to walk with an umbrella and flashlight all night.

The odds are good that this young man would ask me why I had not asked him to go the previous day when he could have used a vehicle. Or he probably would ask if the errand could wait until the next day. But my only response is that he must go and collect the envelope that very night.

Imagine him, walking in the dark, getting soaking wet in the rain, and cursing me. He might curse me even more if he stumbles into some ditches. He will be very upset if his sandal straps break. He will consider that particular trip a real trial. He may even think I purposely allowed him to suffer.

Now assume that before the young man left I told him that, along with the envelope, he would be given a job offer along with visa papers for him to go to one of the countries in the Gulf. Now how will he react during that night trip? He probably won't mind it at all. He might even run to get that envelope. And if he hurts his foot, he would rub it off thinking of the job waiting for him. If he breaks his sandal straps, he would only think of buying a better pair when he has the money.

The Bible says: "Yet what we suffer now is nothing compared to the glory he will give us later" (Romans 8:18). When you know you suffer for a purpose, your entire perspective is different. Remember, the central goal of our life is to glorify God. We cannot glorify God in our own strength. He must empower us by taking away our sinful nature, then giving us what He requires of us.

Dr. John Haggai has taught me his definition of grace: "Grace is God giving us what He requires of us." God requires love of me, but I don't have love. So God has to give me love. Jesus already prayed for us to have God's love in us: "that the mighty love you have for me may be in them" (John 17:26). Similarly, God requires patience of us, but we do not have it. Again God gives us patience by grace. God's grace, freely given to us, can help us change our entire outlook and attitude. It can give us the resources to praise Him, whether in sickness or in good health.

You may say no one could meet your needs. You are wrong. God has more than enough grace to meet your need, no matter what it is.

TRIALS—AND GRACE—COME IN MANY FORMS

When we face trials of many kinds (see James 1:2), we are given God's grace in various forms (see 1 Peter 4:10). It is similar to having a supply of various solutions on hand, each one matching a problem. When the problem arises, the solution can be given out. Our trials are of different magnitude and range, but God's grace is available exactly when and how we need it. We can be sure that God's grace meets us at the place of trials when we get there.

"Dear brothers, is your life full of difficulties and temptations? Then be happy, for when the way is rough, your patience has a chance to grow. So let it grow, and don't try to squirm out of your problems. For when your patience is finally in full bloom, then you will be ready for anything, strong in character, full and complete" (James 1:2–4).

Sometimes difficulties and problems surface in your home and family. They also can be seen in your place of work, in your neighborhood, in your relationship with others, and even in your accomplishments. (You may begin to view the work you do for the kingdom of God as *your* work instead of God's work. You may be emotionally attached to the work and what you unselfishly did.) In facing all these difficulties, God wants you to be "ready for anything, strong in character, full and complete."

OUR RESPONSE TO IRRITATIONS AND INCONVENIENCES

I have had to deal with many different people and with many different personalities in my work. I will never forget one staff member at a hospital where I worked with technical, clinical, nonclinical, and supporting staff. This particular person was the secretarial support for me and the new department. Because of this woman's efficiency, she had been transferred to my department.

At first she seemed to like my way of handling things. But after working with me for two weeks, she began to hate me! I tried to overlook her rude behavior. I thought she might not have worked with a professional with an Indian background before. Perhaps that was the reason she had difficulty getting along. But before long she began to give me serious trouble.

I knew this conflict was not good for the department or the hospital, so I began to handle the woman spiritually. I talked to her about God and the spiritual aspects of life. But her response was just the opposite. She made it clear she didn't like "God talk."

In the beginning she had been so good to me and interested in my plans for setting up a department with good facilities for the hospital. Then she changed, and I found the problem upset me both in my work and in my emotional attitude. Dealing with her constantly while trying to keep up with my work and studies at the theological seminary drained my energy. Finally, I decided to handle the situation diplomatically by moving her to another department with a small increase in pay.

But questions began to rise in my mind. *Why did she hate me? Didn't she see Jesus in me? What kind of Jesus did she see in me if she could hate me?* I really wanted to share some of my spiritual experiences with her and give her the assurance that I was not against her but rather was praying for her. The day before she was to leave my department, I decided to talk to her.

I finished my supper that evening a little earlier than usual in order to spend time in prayer asking God to give me the right words to speak to this woman. I also asked God to prepare her to hear what I had to say and to accept my point of view. But God had other plans! As I prayed, He began to show me things about myself.

God showed me that I had made some serious mistakes during those two initial weeks of working with the staff. According to my cultural background, I was behaving well. I had thought my staff all approved of my way of handling problems and my outlook on life. I thought I was perfectly all right in the ways I dealt with people. But God clearly showed me during my prayer time that I was full of mistakes.

He helped me to see how I had insisted on getting things done by acting superior and condescending. I demanded that things be done my way. This was my first job outside India, and I was used to insisting, demanding, and even raising my voice when I needed things to be done. When I pointed out the mistakes of others, I did so with a sense of superiority. I considered myself the professional and regarded the supporting staff as inferior or lower in status.

I hadn't even responded properly to people's greetings of "Good morning" and "How are you?" Nor did I say "thank you" for the work staff members did. In my mind, it was their job. I never appreciated people for their work. The "problem" woman had worked well at the beginning and had actually done many things that I had not known to do in the new situation. But I never uttered a kind word of appreciation because I simply could not find any reason to do so. In short, I was really not fit to be the leader of the department.

I didn't know the "ABC's" of polished and well-mannered behavior—and I was only handling the supporting staff and the equipment! I hadn't yet started dealing with patients, their relatives, or even with the doctors who send the patients for investigations. So there I was, getting ready to set up and run a new department to handle all medical requests, difficult patients, and anxious relatives in addition to all professional responsibilities. Yet I couldn't even handle my staff.

I thanked God for allowing the conflict with the woman to happen. If it hadn't, I would have been a total failure. Professionally, I had the training I needed to do my job. But I really was not fit to handle my job properly. And the only way I would have known this was when they asked me to leave! But God had allowed that precious woman to help me. She noticed my demanding behavior, my lack of concern, my legalistic way of getting things done, my lack of appreciation for people's work, my self-righteousness. All of these things had been proper and acceptable in India—but they were far from that in my new position.

God can even use unbelievers to show us our drawbacks. And I am grateful that God used that precious woman to polish me before it was too late.

As I went to work the next morning, I knew I had to change. The woman was surprised when I talked to her differently. And she was amazed when I told her that God had used her as a precious tool to shape me and my behavior. She could not understand how God could use her when she was not even a believer! In all humility, I explained to her what happened during the prayer time the previous night. Suddenly she no longer wanted to change departments! Sadly, the arrangements had been made, and she had to leave. But she left as a friend.

Why did God use an unbeliever to change me? Why didn't He use some famous preacher to point out my mistakes? I don't know. But I do know that God has His own ways. He uses both preachers and other people whom He brings into our lives. We need to thank the Lord for all of the people He uses. We need to ask why God has allowed someone to cross our path. Sometimes it is for us to shape them, and sometimes it will be for the purpose of shaping us. Whatever the reason, we can have victory over irritations and unpleasant dealings with people. All we need to do is ask if we caused it or whether we have control over it. If we caused it, we should make things right. If we have control over it, we can, of course, work things out.

Whatever the situation, we can know our God is in all that happens. He is ready to cleanse us if we are wrong. If we are not sure what is wrong with us, God will reveal it and help us correct our mistakes. All we must do is be sensitive and prepared to listen to God.

At clinics for leprosy patients, tests are done by pricking a patient's extremities, such as finger tips, with a pin. If the patient doesn't show much response to the pricking, that means that part of the finger already is affected by leprosy, and so it is no longer sensitive. Some people are no longer sensitive to God's dealings when they are touched by various irritating situations. That is why they later suffer the consequences of their wrong responses of fighting, justifying themselves, or even walking away from their problems.

LIVE WITH ONE ANOTHER AND WITH GOD

One day a person approached me for help and counseling. He was a pastor and a young graduate from the seminary. He was working under a senior pastor who had been helpful to him earlier but now had turned against him. I suggested that he leave that church and serve God elsewhere. He informed me that he had not been given a scholarship by any seminary for his studies, and so finally this pastor offered him a scholarship from the church with the condition that he would serve the church as a junior pastor for five years after he completed his studies.

After working with the senior pastor for three years, the young man told me he would rather die of a heart attack than stay on for another two years. He explained that the senior pastor had been exploiting him all those years, letting him do far too much work. This young pastor would be asked to prepare an article for the monthly bulletin, and when the bulletin was printed the senior pastor would put his own name under that article. He would be asked to prepare sermon outlines for each Sunday, and then the senior pastor modified those outlines and used them as his own messages.

He went on to outline the pastor's rudeness and other bad traits and exploitations. The more he said against the senior pastor, the more angry and hateful he got. He ended his tirade by telling me he was having problems with an ulcer and experienced a lot of fatigue.

It requires a tremendous amount of emotional energy to maintain hatred, bitterness, and resentment. I asked the young man whether he believed in the Bible verse that says "all that happens to us is working for our good" (Romans 8:28). He said he had preached several sermons from the same verse. I asked him whether he agreed to my understanding of this verse, that "all that happens" also included his senior pastor, which would mean that this man whom he hated so much would be of great blessing to him. "He will eventually become good in the end," I said.

The young pastor could not agree that God could be using this senior pastor for his blessing and good future. I asked him whether he had not personally benefited by the preparation, research, and studies involved in writing articles for the bulletin. Had he not benefited in preparing the sermons for all those Sundays?

But he didn't seem to hear me. He just kept on talking

about all the mistakes the senior pastor had made. Finally I told him to accept the senior pastor as a precious person sent by God to shape his character and sharpen his abilities. As a result he must thank the senior pastor and praise God for the man sent by God to bless him for his future ministry. After a long time of discussion, the young pastor agreed to what I had said.

As we prepared to pray together, I asked him to pray for strength to see the senior pastor as a precious person sent by God, and to allow God to change his attitude so that he could really praise God for the older man. We had closed our eyes, but then the young pastor opened his eyes and said: "You say God is using the senior pastor to produce changes in me. Don't you think changes are needed in the senior pastor also?"

That is a mistake we often commit. While God is using someone on us as a tool to change our attitude and character, we are trying to see changes in them or even trying to remove them from the scene. This results in a lot of bitterness and hatred and wrong actions. The junior pastor admitted that when he preached he was trying to preach at the senior pastor indirectly, although he was facing the whole audience. I asked him whether he had succeeded? He said he was a miserable failure and he could not even enjoy his lunch after that sermon because of the cold response from the older pastor!

I told him that while it would be possible for God to use him or someone else to produce changes in the senior man, "in this particular project, God's plan is to see changes in the junior pastor." He began to weep like a child, saying he had been wrong in his behavior. He had never thought of the other man as God's tool to shape his own life and behavior. He confessed his mistakes to God, then went back home. Later he wrote me a letter saying that he was able to be reconciled with his senior pastor without any difficulty. "And," he wrote, "my health has improved."

No wonder! When your attitude is changed and bitterness is gone, your health also improves. I received another letter from the young pastor telling me that he and the senior pastor have a marvelous ministry together in the same church and that God has given him a new senior pastor in the same old man! This senior man also changed his attitude and behavior. The young pastor now talks of his desire to stay and work under that same senior man for another twenty years!

God knows our needs, and He enables us. Remember the woman who had caused me so much trouble at my job? The Christmas after she left my department, I sent some gift items for her children. She came to thank me and to give me a Christmas card. She had purposely purchased a "religious" Christmas card for me, knowing that I am believer in God. There was a picture of the baby Jesus on the card.

I told her we celebrate Christmas to commemorate this first Christmas gift we received about two thousand years ago. God gave the Christmas gift wrapped in the person of Christ. She, too, could receive the gift and become a brand new person inside. Then, once a person became new, he or she could keep on improving their character. I suggested to her that she should unwrap the gift given by God during that year's Christmas season. And she did. She opened the gift she could have received many years earlier when she heard about this gift given at the first Christmas—and she accepted Christ. This gave purpose and meaning to her life.

Have you opened your gift from God? How would your friends or family, who give you gifts wrapped in nice wrapping paper, feel if you left the packet unopened for many years? It would grieve the heart of the giver to see the gift left unopened and uncared for. So it is with God, the greatest Giver of all. He is waiting patiently to see you opening the gift He gave you all those years ago.

When you open this gift of salvation, you will know life's purpose and learn to focus everything on it. God's grace is available to you even before you open yourself to Him. This grace will enable you to face irritating and frustrating situations. Once you understand the purpose of your life, you can focus everything on it and gain a right perspective. You will then be in a position to evaluate all the happenings in light of the values and goals of the kingdom of God.

THE HANDLING OF FAME AND POSITION

My interest has always been twofold: first, to serve as a professional scientist, and second, to serve as a helper in spiritual affairs. When I was actively involved in scientific research, I used to have many opportunities to help people spiritually. Although people are highly educated, I found that they may be suffering from a lot of personal and interpersonal problems.

I was able to share certain spiritual principles with them and help them to change their attitude and live a life of good relationships, dedication to work, and fulfillment.

I have enjoyed the status and the positions associated with my profession. I also have enjoyed the good friendships I have developed among my colleagues. It has been very satisfying to travel to many countries, getting to know people of various backgrounds and sharing with them the importance of the spiritual component in life.

In earlier days I was fully satisfied with a seat in a bus or in the unreserved compartment in the train during my travels. But as my status grew, so did my expectations. Just getting someplace wasn't enough. Soon I was accustomed to first-class travel, and all the benefits that accompany it. Then I tasted international travel, and I began to see that as the most enjoyable kind of travel. For so long I had seen various "lucky" people standing in the line for check-in at the international departure areas. I remember thinking: *Someday I will be flying to go abroad.* When it finally happened, I knew I had arrived.

After a while, though, I reached a point when I began to dislike traveling altogether, in spite of all the special assistance and priority services I received. I was simply tired of travel itself. The round-the-world travel several times a year, staying in different places, even in good and clean hotels, receiving the applause of people—these thing were no longer a thrill.

Nowadays I try to avoid or limit such international trips. I have learned that these are not the important things in life. It is all right to enjoy modern travel facilities, accommodations, and restaurants. But they are not the things that count. What counts is whether or not these things have anything to do with the kingdom of God. That's what is important. I have finally realized that a person is not going to become great by traveling in the first-class section of the plane. Neither will one be diminished by traveling in the third-class compartment of the train!

Of course, it may be difficult for those who are used to one life-style to go down to a lower standard. Honestly, I prefer the comforts to which I am accustomed. However, once in a while I try to check myself by bringing the level of my life-style down.

I still find it difficult to readjust to some things. In the past, for example, I was able to sleep in a room without any ceiling fan in spite of mosquitoes feeding on me. I would only see the rashes of the mosquito bites in the morning. Nowadays, I find sleeping without a fan a little difficult. Even so, though my body and my ego might say no to some readjustments, I know I must be willing to accept whatever the Lord provides for me.

Sometimes He provides a room without a fan and full of mosquitos, and sometimes He provides nice, comfortable, mosquito-proofed and air-conditioned accommodations. I must be willing to accept anything that the Lord gives me—comfort or discomfort, sickness or healing. Whatever the circumstances, I know God's grace is available in the midst of it.

That is where true greatness lies, in seeing everything in the light of the kingdom goal. Whose interest is getting served in your air travel or foreign trip? If it is for your own satisfaction, the thrill will soon be gone. If it is for the kingdom of God, no matter where you are, what you do, or what your position is, you are filling the highest purpose for which you were created.

I have served many well-known and prestigious organizations in many different capacities. But these days I devote my time to two major ministries. The first is my training and counseling ministry in India based at the Navajeevodayam campus in Tiruvalla, Kerala. Both my wife and I help in giving leadership and in looking after the responsibilities assigned to us. There are many people involved in this ministry, and I enjoy working with them— they all do their job as if they are doing their own private ministry. They devote their time with such commitment to the ministry that I don't even need to ask them to do anything. They do everything so well, they inspire me.

The second ministry in which I am involved is the Haggai Institute in Singapore. I met a man of God, Dr. John Haggai, in Atlanta in 1973. Since then our hearts have become closer in the interest of the kingdom of God. I am therefore helping in this ministry of advanced leadership training for Christian leaders from Asia, Africa, and Latin America. This ministry has been going on since 1969, and leaders from one-hundred-ten countries of the Third World have been given advanced training.

This is a month-long training program in the form of an intensive seminar that covers several hours in prayer, devotion, study, discussion, workshop, lectures, and assignments. About sixty to seventy leaders attend at any one time. Because the faculty is chosen from among outstanding leaders of Third World countries, this program is run *by* leaders from the Third World *for* leaders of the Third World.

How do you feel when you are given wonderful opportunities for ministry? I am grateful to God for the privilege of serving Him, and especially through these avenues of service. It has been a learning experience for me, and I am blessed every time I get involved in the ministry. I am thankful to the Lord for the feedback I have received about the blessings people gain through my ministry among them.

I remember the days when I was responsible for the final day graduation program with several visitors and guests at the Institute in Singapore. I used to feel happy and satisfied when I saw a good and successful conclusion. Everything went well because of the hard work of the staff members of Haggai Institute, and yet the people congratulated me for the success of everything. I knew I was facing a problem with all that applause. But I thank God for the message of Dr. John Haggai. One evening he said, "You are dead." I understood that he was telling me I was dead so far as applause was concerned.

Once the program was over, I could really relax and

get a good sleep. Because I was "dead" to the applause—
and the criticism—I didn't spend sleepless time in bed
thinking of what people had said about me. I had no need
to relive everything and to visualize all the great things I
had done. I am glad I received that wonderful message from
that man of God so I could forget the past and think of
further programs for the cause of the kingdom.

Fame, prestige, glory and adulation often are difficult
to handle. Especially when they come suddenly. Few of us,
even the most devoted to our Lord, are able to handle these
things on our own. I knew I was not capable of handling
the unexpected fame and glory I came to receive in my work
and ministry. But God knew this as well, and He met me in
my place of need.

I was returning from a graduation function at Fuller
Seminary School of Missions in 1986 after having received
an award from the school as the "Alumnus of the Year." I
stopped over in Singapore where I heard a man of God
give a fine message. But what struck me hardest was what
he said about Mary, the one who wiped Jesus' feet with
her hair. Mary did not use her hair, the speaker said, because no towel was available. Rather, she had wanted to
use what was glorious to her to serve Jesus. Surely the hair
of a woman is something glorious for her, and Mary used
it in serving Jesus at His feet. Then I realized that all hon-
ors and awards are to be used at the feet of Jesus. Otherwise they have no meaning.

The opportunities I was given to serve were actually
God-given privileges to glorify Him. I was selected to do
certain things, but not because I was great. Nor am I small
and insignificant because I was given substandard accommodations or a small job to do. There is a lot of glamorous
advertisement of preachers and organizations, even in
Christian ministries these days. It may be appropriate in

certain cultures, but it may have a negative effect in other cultures. Sometimes we are asked to sit on the platform during a large meeting, and some other time we may have to sit with the audience. I have learned that it does not matter much where I sit. (In fact, I feel more comfortable when I sit with the audience.) My heart's attitude is more important than where I sit. Outwardly I can be sitting with the audience to show my humility, but at the same time I can be inwardly proud. The Lord looks at the heart.

The motivating factor for what we do in ministry must be spiritual. In most cases, we suffer disappointment when the motivation is other than spiritual. The temporary applause and the resulting ego satisfaction soon vanish. But whenever we can stand behind people and help them minister, we will find they do a much better job than we could do on our own. We all need to recognize the importance of taking the back row and encouraging others to take the front row. What should motivate us all is the constraining love of Christ (see 2 Corinthians 5:14).

When we do things for Christ and His kingdom, there is no need to use what we do to bolster our ego. For example, I had the opportunity to do something in our own training center regarding, among other things, the construction of some buildings. I was emotionally attached to the job until it was completed. Now I have nothing to do with it; my job is completed. I might have spent my wealth and health and a lot of myself on it, but I have no attachment to it. If I am asked not to enter the building that I built, I don't need to feel bad. After its completion, I stood outside and said good-bye to it.

What does that mean? You have to say good-bye to your achievements when your work is done. Recognize that whatever you do is for God's glory, not yours. Otherwise, you will feel terribly insecure. If you really want to stay happy by seeing the fruit of your labor, you need to listen to Jesus: "I must fall and die like a kernel of wheat that falls into the furrows of the earth. Unless I die I will be alone—a single seed. But my death will produce many new wheat kernels—a plentiful harvest of new lives" (John 12:24).

I have learned this important lesson: we must do what we can. Be happy in the fact that you are able to do something. Be happy when others benefit from the fruit of your labor. Rejoice when others get the glory at your expense. After all, you are working for God's glory—and it was from Him that you got your motivation, health, strength, and wealth.

GET THE RIGHT PERSPECTIVE!

When we evaluate everything according to God's kingdom perspective, we realize that our lives will have some impact on the affairs of people around us. When we live as kingdom people, with the values of the kingdom expressed in our dealings, the kingdom will be extended so that many will enjoy the reign of God in their lives. This is called witnessing for Christ, the King who works through our lives, attracting people to enter the kingdom by the new birth. This entry into the kingdom is a free gift. We can present people with the opportunity to enter God's family because of our good testimony for our Lord. We need to get involved in the strengthening of the kingdom, and in the strengthening of the people of God who have entered the kingdom. It is for the kingdom that power is given to God's people to do and bear all things because of Christ, who never ceases to make us able. It is to the kingdom people that Jesus said, "Here on earth you will have many trials and sorrows; but cheer up, for I have overcome the world" (John 16:33).

Kingdom people can have courage in a world of discouragement. Jesus has already made everything we need available to us. We are involved every day in the work of the kingdom. When kingdom people live a holy and God-pleasing life, there will be more justice and peace and brotherhood. Our actions will result in wiping away the tears from the eyes of those who weep with sorrow and suffering. We will be involved in the perfecting of the kingdom, although the final perfecting will take place only when our Lord returns (see Revelation 21:3–4).

I was spending time in prayer and Bible reading on my fiftieth birthday to commit my life afresh for the cause of the kingdom of God. For fifty years I had enjoyed God's air, water, and other resources to maintain my life on this planet. I am grateful to God and the people God used, including my parents, family and friends, for my well-being. But I faced the question of how to occupy my time for the future.

The two words used for time in the New Testament are *"chronos,"* which refers to chronological time, and *"kairos,"* which refers to opportune time. As I considered my past involvement in Christian ministries, I wondered whether I was filling in the time available to me with only those things I personally liked for my own ego satisfaction. Were those the things with which God wanted me to fill my time? By filling it with such good things, I might also have lost the *kairos*, the opportune time. I can easily lose the opportunities for the cause of the kingdom by doing the things I personally like in place of the things God wants me to be doing. The Bible says: "Don't be fools; be wise: make the most of every opportunity you have for doing good" (Ephesians 5:15–16). This was an opportunity for committing myself again to God's way in my life, to fill in the rest of my life with things God wants me to do, and to make use of every opportunity for the cause of the kingdom of God.

Our focus must be on the kingdom of God. We must not disregard the kingdom. God wants to get the work of His kingdom done through me—and through each of His children. At the same time God wants to produce His character in us. Even the adverse things happening to us can be used by God to our advantage, especially to produce His qualities in our lives. What God does through us is very important. We need to be kept as clean and usable channels of blessings to others as God continues to accomplish His purposes for the cause of His kingdom.

12

Epilogue

THE HALL OF FAITH

I have shared our personal experiences with you in the hope that you will be encouraged by what God has done in and through us. God has shown me how vital such encouragement is by using godly people and their lives to encourage and uplift me and my family. I know many people who have gone through even worse situations than ours and emerged victorious. I have had the opportunity to watch, listen to, and learn from several men and women of God who also have received strength from our Lord in facing trials and afflictions.

The most unforgettable such person I have ever met is Dr. John E. Haggai, founder and president of the Haggai Institute. I met this man of God in 1973 in Atlanta, Georgia. I remember the first meeting with him in his office. He shared with me his vision of providing advanced leadership training in culturally relevant evangelism for Christian leaders in Asian, African, and Latin American countries. He wanted to be a blessing to me and to others like me who live in Third World countries. I spent the entire day with him, sharing my concern for my people and the people with whom I come into contact through my profession.

As a scientist, I have seen that science has given us much to help us live. But it can give us nothing to live for.

So many face problems in their family, workplace, and society—and feel incapable of dealing with them. I have felt this same way at times. Dr. Haggai shared some insights with me from his book *How to Win Over Worry*, which I needed very much. Then he took me to his home and introduced me to his wife, Christine, and their only child, Johnny, who was in a wheelchair. Johnny (John Edmund Haggai, Jr.) was twenty-two years old at that time. He was brain-damaged at birth due to a doctor's carelessness during delivery. John Sr. explained how he and his wife were devoting themselves to caring for Johnny; Christine Haggai poured her life into caring for her son. I will never forget the opportunities I had to meet Johnny again before he went to be with the Lord two years later. The suffering that family had endured was unthinkable.

Later on, when John Haggai wrote the book *My Son Johnny*, I realized I had not really known earlier all that the Haggai family had experienced. They had faced personal afflictions and uncertainties. In addition, they had the heavy burden of running a huge advanced leadership training program in Singapore for Christian leaders from Third World countries. This family truly subjected their beliefs to the test of experience.

I saw joy and courage in the Haggai family, in spite of all the discouraging circumstances. I am grateful God brought this family into my path, for they have been a great encouragement to me. In addition to sharing with John Haggai on a personal level, God has given me opportunities to listen to uplifting messages he has delivered. I saw, time and again, how the Haggai family received strength from God and so refused to let fear and disappointments defeat them.

Since Johnny's death, I have seen the Haggais' positive response to further sicknesses. Their attitude and application of the principles in God's Word sustain them. Few would imagine that they are going through such afflictions.

Another person who has been of great encouragement to us is a fellow scientist, Dr. DeLores E. Johnson. An outstanding specialist in nuclear medicine, Dr. Johnson was professor of medicine at the University of California School of Medicine and chief of nuclear medicine at Harbor General Hospital at Torrance, California. She has made outstanding contributions in science and at the same time has encouraged many fellow scientists to consider seriously the spiritual components in life.

And yet, in the midst of her wonderful professional and spiritual contributions, I have watched her suffer from a multitude of physical problems. She must use a wheelchair or walk slowly using a cane. Her entire body has aches and pains. She had to undergo surgery several times for joints, muscles, and even her eyes. Though she has suffered unbearable pain, Dr. Johnson is always cheerful and helpful. The other scientists who know her see her as a living miracle. They know she has something that many people do not have. What a difference God's grace makes in life!

I was encouraged by this lady's life, attitude, and response to adverse situations. Some who know her have asked why such things have happened to her when she has done so much good for God and for other people. But she has no such questions. She simply praises God at all times for all things. People who hear her voice over the telephone would never know that she is suffering physically. God has given her gracious words to encourage people in times of their discouragements. When I need encouragement to bear the sickness of my children or to bear the uncertainties of pain and difficulty, I give Dr. DeLores Johnson a call.

Another person who has challenged and encouraged

me is Clayton Douglas, a fellow scientist in nuclear medicine and radiological physics. He, too, has made outstanding contributions in nuclear medicine and was once president of the California chapter of the Society of Nuclear Medicine. His hard work challenged me. Nothing could defeat him. He almost died from a serious illness. Once we all gathered to pray earnestly for his recovery from surgery. He worked at St. Mary's Hospital in Long Beach for a number of years in the nuclear medicine and radiology department and is now working in Portland, Oregon. He did not give up when sickness and trials began to overcome him. I saw him working with his own hands in the laboratory and machine shops, developing new procedures and methods in radiological investigations and therapy. When he is not in the laboratory, he is working in his garden growing fruit and vegetables. What an encouragement such people of God are, people who refuse to surrender to their circumstances, people who have taken the spiritual components into consideration and applied them in their own lives.

Dr. Dwight Carlson of Rolling Hills, California, is another person in the medical field who has taught me marvelous lessons. He was chairman of the board of the Rolling Hills Covenant Church. He also was a specialist in internal medicine, and he did studies in psychiatry. His brother (Dr. Paul Carlson) was a committed missionary doctor in Zaire (then Congo), and was martyred there during the Congo crisis. Now Dwight and his dear wife, Betty, are helping their daughter Susan deal with blood cancer. And yet, their attitude is so marvelous and encouraging.

I have been immensely blessed talking with Dwight and Betty and reading what they have written. This entire family and all they have faced through these afflictions, suffering, trials, and unexpected experiences in life are

God's special encouraging channels. And, as they will tell you themselves, the thing that has made the difference in their lives, that has kept them from being defeated, is the spiritual component.

Another special teacher of theological truths has been the Rev. Richard Bowie, former principal of Bishops College, Calcutta, and currently director of training at the Haggai Institute in Singapore. Richard and his wife, Audrey, gave me something I could not get from theological books. They are experiencing difficulties similar to what we have experienced. Their only son, Jonathan, has been sick since birth. Jonathan is in a wheelchair. He needs constant assistance, although he is in his teenage years, and it seems there is no known medical cure for the illness that plagues him. The words the Bowies speak, the attitude they show, are so valuable to us who face discouragements. They are happy because God is active in their lives. They believe in God's healing power, but they have accepted Jonathan's situation and they are looking after him as God's calling. In the years I have known them, I have never seen any sort of disappointment or bitterness or anxiety in their lives. I praise God for bringing such people in my path during many years.

Sister Saramma Thomas is another blessing. She gave her life for the cause of the kingdom of God. Involved in women's ministry in Kerala, she suffered painful and heartbreaking experiences, both mentally and physically, because of misunderstandings and illnesses. Yet she victoriously presented messages from God's Word every time she came out of some afflicting experience. She inspired me and many others with her sustaining power.

Mrs. Alice Chua, of Singapore, was an active, energetic woman who worked faithfully for the cause of the kingdom of God. Then she had a stroke. I saw her surmounting her limitations through the power of God. Being bedridden and then limited to a wheelchair did not stop her. She kept working. Now she is able to walk with a cane, and she continues her ministry of bringing people of many nationalities together, introducing them to each other, and providing opportunities for fellowship and strength in the Lord. She has blessed many lives. She never allowed discouragement to defeat her.

Mrs. Annamma Matthew of Mavelikara, Kerala, challenged me with her positive attitude despite sickness and disability. She was bedridden because of old age and sickness for a number of years. She told me that Jesus already had gone through more suffering than she would ever face. "It is like going over a very thin bridge sometimes," she said, "a bridge made of thread! It involves a lot of risk going over it. But our Lord already went across a bridge just like this before us, and so we can follow Him."

She went on to tell me about the design of bridges and the ways in which engineers calculate the load a bridge can handle. She explained that bridges designed for light vehicles would not be used for trains to cross. Similarly, God knows our limits. He knows how much burden, pain, and affliction we each can carry. God is the "master engineer."

My grandparents and parents were an inspiration to me, too. As they raised me, I saw demonstrated in them the courage to face adverse situations. Similarly, my wife had the privilege of being brought up by believing and committed parents. Our parents gave us something money cannot buy: a foundation of faith in God. What a wonderful environment we had in which to grow up.

I remember a time when I was young and discouraged over something. My father encouraged me, relating a time when he had faced a similar disappointment. He had applied for a job as a clerk and had not gotten it. As a result, he decided to pursue studies in electrical engineering—and ended up working as an electrical engineer. Had he gotten the job he originally wanted, he would have remained a clerk. (In our country, once a clerk, always a clerk, in most cases!) He helped me to see how our disappointments can be God's appointments.

My father-in-law, too, was a man of God who applied biblical principles in his daily life. There were many occasions when he was tempted to compromise his principles because of various kinds of pressures. But he chose to suffer rather than give up those principles. He counted it a joy to suffer disadvantages because of standing firm on the principles of God's Word. It was encouraging to me to see how he was able to be victorious despite sufferings caused by the corrupt world around him.

These stories of godly, victorious people could go on and on. And each one is a wonderful encouragement that we all can turn the worst circumstances into the best, with God's help.